# Weavers

William K. Durr
Jean M. LePere
Rita M. Bean
Nicholas A. Glaser
Ruth Hayek Brown

*Consultant:*
**Hugh Schoephoerster**

**HOUGHTON MIFFLIN COMPANY**     **BOSTON**
Atlanta  Dallas  Geneva, Illinois  Hopewell, New Jersey  Palo Alto  Toronto

# Acknowledgments

Grateful acknowledgment is given for the contributions of Paul McKee.

For each of the selections listed below, grateful acknowledgment is made for permission to adapt and/or reprint copyrighted material, as follows:

"All Except Sammy," adapted from *All Except Sammy,* by Gladys Yessayan Cretan. Copyright © 1966 by Gladys Yessayan Cretan. Used by permission of Little, Brown and Company.

"Annie and the Old One," adapted from *Annie and the Old One,* by Miska Miles. Copyright © 1971 by Miska Miles. Used by permission of Little, Brown and Company.

"Beauty," from *I am a Pueblo Indian Girl,* by E-Yeh-Shure'. Copyright 1939 by William Morrow & Company, Inc. Reprinted by permission of the publisher.

"Brave Janet of Reachfar," from *Brave Janet Reachfar,* by Jane Duncan. Copyright © 1975 by Jane Duncan. Used by permission of Houghton Mifflin/Clarion Books, and A. M. Heath & Company Ltd., agents for The Jane Duncan Estate.

"A Cane in Her Hand," adapted from *A Cane in Her Hand,* by Ada B. Litchfield. Text copyright © 1977 by Ada B. Litchfield. Reprinted by permission of Albert Whitman & Company.

"Coplas," from *Coplas, Folk Poems in Spanish and English,* collected by Toby Talbot. Text copyright © 1972 by Toby Talbot. Reprinted by permission of Four Winds Press, a Division of Scholastic Magazines, Inc., the author, and her agents, Raines & Raines.

"Dance of the Animals," from the book *The Tiger and the Rabbit and Other Tales,* by Pura Belpré. Copyright © 1977, 1965, 1946, 1944 by Pura Belpré. Used by permission of the author.

"The Dancers," adaptation of *The Dancers,* by Walter Dean Myers. Text copyright © 1972 by Walter Dean Myers. Used by permission of Parents' Magazine Press.

"The Fastest Quitter in Town," adapted from *The Fastest Quitter in Town,* by Phyllis Green. Copyright © 1972 by Phyllis Green. A Young Scott Book. Used by permission of Addison-Wesley Publishing Company, Inc.

"The Gift of Corn," adapted text and six illustrations from *Corn Is Maize: The Gift of the Indians*, written and illustrated by Aliki. Copyright © 1976 by Aliki Brandenberg. A Let's-Read-and-Find-Out Book. Used by permission of Thomas Y. Crowell.

"Grandmother's Corn," from *Three Stalks of Corn*, by Leo Politi. Copyright © 1976 by Leo Politi. Reprinted by permission of Charles Scribner's Sons.

"The Great Cleanup," an excerpt from *The Mushroom Center Disaster*, by N. M. Bodecker. A Margaret K. McElderry Book. Copyright © 1974 by N. M. Bodecker. Used by permission of Atheneum Publishers.

"In Which Pooh and Piglet Go Hunting and Nearly Catch a Woozle," from *Winnie-The-Pooh*, by A. A. Milne. Copyright 1954 by A. A. Milne. Reprinted by permission of the publishers, E. P. Dutton, and Methuen Children's Books Ltd. Also used by permission of Curtis Brown Ltd. on behalf of the Estate of E. H. Shepard.

"Josephine's 'Magination," from *Josephine's 'Magination*, written and illustrated by Arnold Dobrin. Copyright © 1973 by Arnold Dobrin. Reprinted by permission of Four Winds Press, a Division of Scholastic Magazines, Inc.

"Knowing Your 9's," from *The Great Perpetual Learning Machine*, by Jim Blake and Barbara Ernst. Copyright © 1976 by Jim Blake and Barbara Ernst. Used by permission of Little, Brown and Company.

"Lewis Has a Trumpet," from *In the Middle of the Trees*, by Karla Kuskin. Copyright © 1958 by Karla Kuskin. Used by permission of Harper & Row, Publishers, Inc.

"The Lion," by Dusan Radovic. From *The UNICEF Book of Children's Poems*, compiled by William K. Kaufman; adapted for English-reading children by Joan Gilbert Van Poznac. © 1970 by Stackpole Books. Used by permission.

"The Magic Pumpkin," from *The Magic Pumpkin*, by Gloria Skurzynski. Copyright © 1971 by Gloria Skurzynski. Reprinted by permission of Four Winds Press, a Division of Scholastic Magazines, Inc.

"Magic Words to Feel Better." Text by Edward Field from *Songs and Stories of the Netsilik Eskimo*, part of the upper elementary school course, *Man, a Course of Study*, developed by the Social Studies Program of EDC under a grant from the National Science Foundation. Text copyright © 1967, 1968 Education Development Center, Inc. Used by permission.

"Musical Pets," by Leona Meals. Reprinted from *Ranger Rick's Nature Magazine*, by permission of the publisher, the National Wildlife Federation.

"Penny Savings Bank," by Ruth Morris Graham. Originally appeared in the May 1976 edition of *Cricket* Magazine. Used by permission of the author.

"Petronella," adaptation of *Petronella*, by Jay Williams. Text copyright © 1973 by Jay Williams. Used by permission of Parents' Magazine Press, and Russell & Volkening, Inc.

(Acknowledgments and Artist Credits are continued on page 368.)

# Contents

# Weavers

MAGAZINE ONE

# Contents

# The Fastest Quitter in Town

by PHYLLIS GREEN

The pitcher began the wind-up. He threw the ball to home plate. Crack! The batter hit a grounder. The shortstop scooped it up. He threw it to Johnny Colmer.

"Easy out, Johnny," he yelled.

Johnny touched one foot on first base, ready to make the catch. He knew he had it! But the only thing he caught was . . . air!

Johnny threw down his mitt. "I quit!" he said.

Everybody started yelling, "You always quit when you do something stupid! Why don't you learn to catch?"

Johnny yelled back, "I *can* catch. Old Gromering can't throw."

"Come on. Let's play without him. We don't need him," the boys said.

Johnny picked up his mitt and ran off the field. When he got to the edge of the schoolyard, he sat down on the curb.

Tears made paths down his dusty cheeks. He felt awful. He had promised himself that he would play the whole game today. But he had quit right at the start.

Johnny got up and wiped his face on his shirt. They would never let him back in the game. He decided to see Great-Grandfather and tell him about Gromering's bad throw.

Johnny Colmer lived with his parents at 1206 Fifth Street. His grandparents lived next door. Someone else lived there too — Johnny's great-grandfather. He was ninety years old.

Great-Grandfather's eyes had become very bad. He could hardly see anything. But he had lots of good stories to tell. He told Johnny about the first automobiles, and about days when there was no television, and how nobody talked in the first movies.

When Johnny arrived, the first thing Great-Grandfather said was, "Short game today?"

Johnny didn't say anything.

"I thought you were going to play the whole game today. Something go wrong?" asked Great-Grandfather.

"Yeah," said Johnny.

"I see," Great-Grandfather said. "Well, do you suppose your grandmother has any cookies hidden away from us?"

It was hard for Great-Grandfather to get up, but Johnny helped him. Then Johnny got the cookies from the top of the refrigerator.

"Get yourself some milk," Great-Grandfather said. "Then tell me about today. Someone break the rules?"

"No," Johnny said. "Just Joe Gromering. He thinks he's so hot. Only he never learned to throw a ball."

"That so?" said Great-Grandfather. "He's that bad, huh?"

"He's not *real* bad. Just throws a little high."

"That's why you quit? You missed the ball?"

"Not exactly. I mean, kind of. Well, tomorrow I'm going to play the whole game no matter what those stupid guys do."

Great-Grandfather patted his shoulder. "Tomorrow you'll be ready for him. Tomorrow you'll catch the ball. But Johnny, if by some chance you miss it, don't give up. Keep playing. It's a game. You're supposed to have fun."

The next afternoon, Johnny took his mitt. He walked over to the schoolyard. "Oh, no," the boys groaned. "Here comes Colmer, the fastest quitter in town."

Johnny stood around just hitting his mitt while the other boys played.

Finally one boy called, "All right, Colmer. We'll give you one more chance. Are you going to play the whole game today?"

"Yeah," said Johnny.

"Okay. Get out in left field."

In the third inning, when Johnny went to bat, he hit the ball far into center field. It looked like a homer. He ran fast. As he turned third base, he saw the ball moving toward the plate.

"Slide!" someone yelled.

He slid!

He got up smiling and brushed the dirt off his pants. He was sure he was safe by a hair.

"Out!" someone yelled.

"I'm safe!" Johnny shouted.

"You're out!" they yelled.

Johnny tried not to say anything, but suddenly the words came out.

"I quit."

Everybody began to scream and yell, "That was your last chance, Colmer. You're off the team for good. Don't come around ever again."

Johnny went straight to see Great-Grandfather. But he didn't tell him about the game because the old man was very upset.

"What's the matter, Great-Grandpa?" Johnny asked.

"Oh, Johnny," the old man said, "thank goodness you've come. I need your eyes. You know
my ring, the gold one with the real diamond in the
center? The one my dear Nancy gave me? She
was your great-grandmother, Johnny. And I've
lost the ring she gave me."

"I'll find it," said Johnny.

Johnny crawled under Great-Grandfather's
bed. He pulled up the pillow on his favorite
chair. He looked through Great-Grandfather's
pillowcase and sheets and blankets to see if the
ring had fallen off his finger while he slept. He
looked everywhere, and Great-Grandfather en-
couraged him.

"Look in the window seat, Johnny, and under the rug, and on the television table. It was just a small diamond, but it was real. And Nancy gave it to me."

But Johnny couldn't find it.

Johnny looked for the ring again the next day. He looked every day for a week. But he did not find the ring.

"I've got to find that ring, Johnny. I promised I'd never take it off. Now I've lost it."

"It's not your fault," Johnny said. "It must have fallen off. You can't help that."

But each day the old man got more disturbed. He fussed a lot and cried a lot. Johnny's parents were very worried.

One day Mrs. Colmer said, "I bought a ring just like his at the dime store. Johnny, give it to him and maybe he'll think it's his ring. He'll never know. He can't see anything any more."

"But I can't," Johnny said. "He *will* know! He's not stupid. He wants the ring with the real diamond in it."

"Johnny, if we thought it would help, we would *buy* him a good ring with a little diamond in it. But he's a very old man. He forgets easily. He would probably lose it too."

"Okay," Johnny said, "but he'll know it isn't his ring."

Johnny went to see Great-Grandfather. He closed the door to the room so no one would hear. He put the ring in Great-Grandfather's hand.

"Johnny," he said, "that's not my ring."

"I know, Great-Grandpa. But Mom and Dad and Grandma and Grandpa are all upset because you're upset over losing the diamond ring. They want you to think this is your ring and to be happy again. Can you pretend it's your ring? And I promise if your ring can be found, I will find it. I will never give up."

"Do you mean you won't quit on me? Okay, Johnny. I'll pretend."

For almost a month, Johnny didn't go near the schoolyard when the boys were playing ball. He was busy with his promise to Great-Grandfather. He looked and looked. Each day when he woke up, he always felt it would be the special day when he would find the ring.

But it never was.

One day when Johnny went to see Great-Grandfather, the old man said, "Johnny, I feel like a little sun. Help me out to the porch."

"You haven't been out for a long time, Great-Grandpa."

"Well, when you get old, you'll find out, Johnny, it's just easier to stay inside on your favorite chair and snooze."

They sat on the porch together. Johnny looked at the backyard. "Great-Grandpa, were you out here on the day you lost your ring?"

The old man bent his head to one side. "I don't know. It's so hard to remember anymore."

"Maybe you were. I've looked everywhere else."

Great-Grandfather got excited. "Johnny, sometimes when I'm out here, I walk over to the rock garden to touch the marigolds and zinnias. I can't see them too well, but I like to touch them. Look over there, Johnny. I've got a feeling."

Johnny crawled through the grass, looking, looking. He came to the rock garden. He parted the marigolds and touched the earth around their stems. He felt around the edges of the rocks. He separated the red and yellow zinnias and looked

through their leaves. He saw something near a zinnia stem — something shiny.

"Great-Grandpa!" he yelled. "I found it!" He took the ring to his great-grandfather.

Tears came to the old man's eyes. He felt the lost ring. It was caked with dirt.

"You found my ring. Thank you, Johnny. I don't know what I would have done without you."

The whole family was thrilled. Johnny's grandmother put tape around the ring. Now it would fit Great-Grandfather's finger better and not fall off again.

And Johnny felt so good inside. It was such a good feeling to have found the ring. He hadn't given up. He hadn't even wanted to quit. The ring was so important to Great-Grandfather, he *never* would have quit.

The next day, he went around to the school-yard. The boys all laughed when they saw him. "Well, look who's here," they said.

"How about one more chance?" Johnny asked.

The boys hooted and laughed. "For Colmer, the quitter?" they said.

Johnny smiled. "For Colmer, the fastest hitter in town," he said.

One boy said, "I vote no on the quitter."

Other boys shouted, "No! He's a quitter."

But Gromering yelled, "C'mon, you guys. You know we need another player. Get over on third base, Johnny."

Johnny ran to third before they could change their minds.

It was after supper when he dropped in to see Great-Grandfather.

"Where have you been, Johnny? You're so late today. I thought you forgot about me."

"I was playing ball," said Johnny. "Can't you guess why I'm so late, Great-Grandpa?"

"Well, let's see," Great-Grandfather said, trying to remember.

"Great-Grandpa, I used to be a quitter! But today I didn't quit. And I feel great."

"You a quitter?" Great-Grandfather asked. "That doesn't seem possible. Not my Johnny. Let's go get some cookies."

Johnny helped the old man into the kitchen. They ate chocolate-chip cookies that Johnny's grandmother had made that day.

Great-Grandfather said, "You came late today. Where have you been?"

Johnny looked at his great-grandfather. He reached over and touched the lines in the old man's face. They were so deep. "I was playing baseball, Great-Grandpa."

"Did you win, Johnny?"

"No, we lost," Johnny said. "Boy, did we ever lose! Twenty to seven. But I got two home runs."

"I wish I could have seen you make those home runs. Well, I'm so tired, I better get to bed," Great-Grandfather said.

Johnny helped him back to his room.

"Good-night, Great-Grandpa," Johnny said. He kissed his forehead. "And thanks. Thanks a lot."

"Don't thank me," Great-Grandfather said. "Your grandmother made the cookies. See you tomorrow."

## AUTHOR

Writing stories is only one of Phyllis Green's many interests. She has been a third-grade teacher, a special-education teacher, a singer with a band, and an actress. Her latest hobby is tap dancing. Mrs. Green and her husband and two children live in Wisconsin and enjoy traveling.

*The Fastest Quitter in Town* was Mrs. Green's first children's book. She has also written poems, short stories, and magazine articles. Two of her other books, *Ice River* and *Wild Violets,* are also about problems children meet in growing up.

# Lewis Has a Trumpet

by KARLA KUSKIN

A trumpet
A trumpet
Lewis has a trumpet
A bright one that's yellow
A loud proud horn.
He blows it in the evening
When the moon is newly rising
He blows it when it's raining
In the cold and misty morn
It honks and it whistles
It roars like a lion
It rumbles like a lion
With a wheezing huffing hum
His parents say it's awful
Oh really simply awful
But
Lewis says he loves it
It's such a handsome trumpet
And when he's through with trumpets
He's going to buy a drum.

# Something Strange Is Going On

by ELIZABETH LEVY

One day Jill came home, and Fletcher wasn't there.

Jill asked Linda, the woman who took care of her during the day, "Have you seen Fletcher?"

"He was sitting out there on the front steps around lunch time," said Linda.

"You haven't seen him since?" asked Jill.

"I haven't looked for him," said Linda.

Jill went outside to look around. She ran into her friend, Gwen. "Hey," she said, "I can't find Fletcher."

"What do you mean?" asked Gwen. "Your dog never needs finding. He never goes anywhere."

"That's just the point," said Jill. "He wasn't in front of the house when I got home."

Every day when Jill came home, Fletcher got up off the front steps and wagged his tail. This was exercise to Fletcher.

"Maybe something strange is going on," said Gwen. "Maybe somebody snatched Fletcher." She began to tap the braces on her teeth.

"Don't be silly," said Jill. "What would somebody want Fletcher for?"

"I don't know, but it seems strange to me."

"Look, I know you love mysteries, but that doesn't help me find Fletcher," said Jill.

"We'll get to the bottom of this. I'll help you," said Gwen.

All afternoon Gwen and Jill searched for Fletcher.

By evening Jill was really worried. When her mother came home from work, Jill told her that Fletcher was missing.

Suddenly Jill started to cry.

"It'll be all right," said her mother. "A dog like Fletcher can't go far. I'll call the police."

The police said that nobody had called in about a funny-looking dog with a big stomach.

At school the next day, Gwen asked Jill if there was any news.

"He's been gone all night," said Jill. "He never came home."

During Math class, Jill got the feeling that Fletcher was home safe. She was sure of it.

As soon as school was over, Jill and Gwen ran to Jill's house.

Fletcher wasn't there.

"The police are not going to find Fletcher," said Gwen. "We have to make a house-to-house search and ask if anybody has seen him."

"Not everybody knows what Fletcher looks like," said Jill.

"You're right!" said Gwen. "Get some paper and crayons."

Jill and Gwen each made drawings of Fletcher. Then they were ready to begin the search.

The first house that they came to was the Hollanders'.

"It's an awfully cute little drawing," said Mr. Hollander. "Which of you girls did it?"

"I did," said Jill. "But have you seen Fletcher?"

"How long has he been missing?" asked Mr. Hollander.

"Since yesterday," said Gwen.

"Well, don't worry. My dog goes away for days. But he comes back."

As soon as he closed the door, Gwen said, "Why was he in such a hurry to tell us that his dog runs away all the time?"

"Because he does," said Jill. "He's that huge German shepherd."

"I think that man's hiding something," said Gwen.

At the next house, they showed Mrs. Duga the picture. "How pretty!" she said.

"Thank you," said Jill. "Have you seen him by any chance?"

"Now let's see," said Mrs. Duga. "I saw him a few days ago sitting on your front steps."

"But have you seen him since yesterday?" asked Gwen.

"I don't think so," said Mrs. Duga.

As they walked away, Gwen said, "Mrs. Duga went out of her way to tell us she saw Fletcher a couple of days ago — WHY?"

It went on that way all day. Every place they went, Gwen found something that seemed not quite right. The one thing Gwen could not find was Fletcher.

Late in the afternoon, they came to a big house that belonged to Fiedler Fernbach. Mr. Fernbach was the most famous person in the neighborhood because he made television commercials.

Mr. Fernbach himself opened the door. "Hi there," he said. "What can I do for you girls?"

"My name is Jill, and this is Gwen," said Jill. "My dog is lost, and we're asking everybody if they've seen him."

"NOPE!" said Mr. Fernbach. "Never saw him in my life!"

He started to close the door. . . .

"But, Mr. Fernbach," said Gwen, sticking her foot in the door, "you don't even know what he looks like."

"Well . . . er . . . heh, heh . . ." said Mr. Fernbach, turning pink.

"Here's a picture," said Jill.

"Oh," said Mr. Fernbach, hardly looking at the picture. "Just as I thought, I haven't seen him."

He shut the door with a BANG!

"Now this time I'm sure," said Gwen as they left. "Fernbach said he'd never seen Fletcher *before* he looked at our picture."

31

"So?" said Jill.

"How could he say he'd never seen Fletcher if he didn't know what Fletcher looked like?"

Jill stared at Gwen. "You know," she said. "You really *have* something!"

"See!" exclaimed Gwen. "SOMETHING STRANGE IS GOING ON!"

"Fernbach could only know what Fletcher looks like if he *has* Fletcher," said Jill. "But what would Fernbach want Fletcher for?"

"That's what we've got to find out," said Gwen. "We've got to watch his every move. We'll meet in the morning and follow him."

"How?" asked Jill. "He'll go to work in his car. Besides, we've got to go to school."

Gwen played with her braces. It was a problem. Finally she said, "Maybe your mother can help."

That night, Jill told her mother everything.

"Let me get this straight," said Jill's mother. "Fernbach said he had never seen Fletcher before he even looked at the drawing, and Fernbach slammed the door on you?"

Jill nodded her head.

"Now, you want me to skip work tomorrow and follow Fernbach?" asked Jill's mother.

"Gwen and I want to go with you," said Jill. "You have to ask her parents to let her come. You also have to write a note to get us out of school."

"Well," said Jill's mother, "I don't know what I'll tell my boss, and I'll look silly if Fernbach catches me — but I'll do it."

They all met early next morning. They drove to Fernbach's house and sat where they were hidden by a big tree.

The garage door went up.

Jill's mother started her car as quietly as she could. When Fernbach moved . . . she was ready.

Finally, Fernbach stopped in front of a big building.

"He's just going to work," said Jill. "The whole thing's a joke."

"Come on," said Jill's mother. "We're going to get to the bottom of this."

Inside, a woman at the desk asked, "Can I help you?"

"We have business with Mr. Fernbach," said Jill's mother with a big smile.

"Go right in," said the woman, pointing to a big door marked PRIVATE. They went in.

They found themselves in a long hall with lots of doors. Just then, they saw Fernbach go through a door at the end of the hall. (Luckily, Fernbach did not see them.)

"Let's go," whispered Gwen.

"It's now or never," whispered Jill's mother.

Jill opened the door. It was a big room, full of movie equipment and bright lights. In the middle, with a big can of dog food by his side, lay Fletcher!

"HOW DARE YOU COME IN WHEN WE'RE SHOOTING!" shouted Fernbach.

Jill ran to Fletcher, who got up and wagged his tail.

"That's the first time I've seen that dog move!" said a man with a camera.

"YOU STOLE JILL'S DOG!" yelled Gwen, pointing at Fernbach.

"I saw him on the street," Fernbach stuttered. "He got up and followed me, and I didn't know whose dog he was."

"You're a liar!" said Gwen.

"Yeah," said Jill. "Fletcher didn't follow you because he never follows anyone."

"Mr. Fernbach," said Jill's mother, "I don't think you're telling the truth. You took Fletcher, and I want to know why."

"I'll tell you why," said the man with the camera. "Your dog is a natural for TV. I've never seen a dog lie so still. Besides, he's got a nice smile. Fernbach would have had to pay a lot of money to use your dog. That's why he took him."

Fiedler Fernbach looked as if he wanted to cry. "Please don't call the police," he whined. "I'll pay you the money. Your dog is really perfect for this commercial. He'll be famous."

Gwen and Jill and her mother went into a corner.

"I think Fernbach's going to cry," said Jill, looking over her shoulder.

"I don't know whether we can prove that Fletcher didn't follow him," said Jill's mother. "I'm not sure the police can do anything."

"Maybe you should let Fernbach do the commercial and make him pay you," said Gwen.

"I wouldn't want to make Fletcher a star, but maybe one commercial . . ." said Jill's mother.

"I really don't want to see Fernbach cry," said Jill.

"Well, we're agreed," said Jill's mother. "We'll let him do this one commercial."

Jill's mother told Fernbach that they had decided not to call the police.

"Oh, thank you! THANK YOU! I know you'll love the way he looks in the commercial!" said Fernbach, trembling with relief.

The first day the commercial was on TV, Jill and her mother took part of the money Fletcher had earned and gave a big party.

Fletcher paid for everything. All through the party, he lay on the front steps smiling, except when the commercial was on. . . . At that moment, Fletcher was asleep.

## AUTHOR

Elizabeth Levy has written several popular stories about Jill and Gwen, the clever girl detectives. One of them, *Something Queer at the Ball Park,* was chosen as a Junior Literary Guild selection. Two of her other books for older readers have also received honors.

After going to college in New York City, Ms. Levy wrote scripts for educational films and was an editor for a book publisher. She has also done research for a large broadcasting company.

# Following Directions

There are many times when it is important to be able to understand and follow directions. These times may be when you are making something, playing a new game, or learning to do something. Then you will need to do exactly what the directions tell you.

Sometimes you read directions, and sometimes someone tells them to you. When you are reading, be sure that you read *all* the directions carefully before you start to do anything. Then read the directions again to make sure that you understand all the steps and the order in which they should be followed.

If someone is telling you directions, you should listen carefully. If there is anything you do not understand, ask about it, but wait until the person is finished giving the directions. Something that is said later may explain a step you didn't understand before. Don't be afraid to ask questions. If you don't understand all the steps, you may do something wrong.

Here is a story about a girl who was learning how to make something and the problems she had following directions:

Bernie was teaching Bonnie how to make French toast. Bonnie was in a hurry. She was hungry.

"First, you need a mixing bowl, a fork, and a frying pan," Bernie said slowly.

"Done," said Bonnie.

"Now, to make eight slices of French toast, you need two eggs, a dash of cinnamon and sugar, half a teaspoon of salt, and two thirds of a cup of milk," said Bernie.

"Okay, but don't I need bread? It's French *toast,* you know," Bonnie pointed out.

"Don't rush me," Bernie complained. "I was going to say eight slices of bread next, also two tablespoons of butter."

"Sorry," said Bonnie.

"Now put the eggs, milk, cinnamon, sugar, and salt into the bowl. Use the fork to beat them until they're foamy. Melt the butter in the frying pan over a medium flame. Then dip a slice of bread in the egg mixture, and brown the slice on each side in the frying pan. . . . Hey!" Bernie yelped.

Bonnie had stuck a plain piece of bread in the buttered frying pan and was pouring the egg mixture over it. "I figured this way was faster," she said. "I'm so hungry!"

"But that's wrong!" cried Bernie. He looked at the mess in the frying pan. "I was hungry too," he moaned. "Now I've lost my appetite."

Bonnie nodded sadly. "Me too," she said.

What does Bonnie have to learn about following directions? Yes, she should listen carefully and ask questions *after* the person has finished giving directions. She should also follow the steps in order and not try to take shortcuts.

## REVIEW

1. When will you need to understand and follow directions?
2. Why should you read directions a second time?
3. What should you do if you are listening to someone give directions and there is something you do not understand?
4. In the story, Bonnie learned the importance of following steps in order. Why is it important to do that?

## READING TO FOLLOW DIRECTIONS

See if you can answer the following questions about making French toast:

1. What utensils (like pots and pans) do you need to make French toast?
2. What ingredients (like food and seasonings) do you need to make French toast?
3. How many eggs do you need? How much milk? How much butter?
4. List the steps in the order you should follow them to make French toast. The last step mentioned in the directions is to put a slice of bread in the buttered frying pan.

# Petronella

by JAY WILLIAMS

In the kingdom of Skyclear Mountain, three princes were always born to the king and queen. The oldest prince was always called Michael, the middle prince was always called George, and the youngest was always called Peter. When they were grown, they always went out to seek their fortunes. What happened to the oldest prince and the middle prince no one ever knew. But the youngest prince always rescued a princess, brought her home, and in time ruled over the kingdom. That was the way it had always been. And so far as anyone knew, that was the way it would always be.

Until now.

*Now* was the time of King Peter the twenty-sixth and Queen Blossom. An oldest prince was born, and a middle prince. But the youngest prince turned out to be a girl.

"Well," said the king gloomily, "we can't call her Peter. We'll have to call her Petronella. And what's to be done about it, I'm sure I don't know."

There was nothing to be done. The years passed, and the time came for the princes to go

out and seek their fortunes. Michael and George
said good-by to the king and queen and mounted
their horses. Then out came Petronella. She was
dressed in traveling clothes, with her bag packed
and a sword by her side.

"If you think," she said, "that I'm going to sit
at home, you are mistaken. I'm going to seek my
fortune too."

"Impossible!" said the king.

"What will people say?" cried the queen.

"Look," said Prince Michael. "Be reasonable,
Pet. Stay home. Sooner or later a prince will
turn up here."

Petronella smiled. She was a tall, handsome
girl with flaming red hair, and when she smiled
in that particular way, it meant she was trying to
keep her temper.

"I'm going with you," she said. "I'll find a

prince if I have to rescue one from something myself. And that's that."

The grooms brought out her horse. She said good-by to her parents, and away she went behind her two brothers.

They traveled into the flatlands below Skyclear Mountain. After many days, they entered a great dark forest. They came to a place where the road divided into three, and there at the fork sat a little, wrinkled old man covered with dust and spiderwebs.

"Where do these roads go, old man?" inquired Prince Michael.

"The road on the right goes to the city of Gratz," the man replied. "The road in the center goes to the castle of Blitz. The road on the left goes to the house of Albion the enchanter. And that's one."

"What do you mean by 'And that's one'?" asked Prince George.

"I mean," said the old man, "that I am forced to sit on this spot without stirring and that I must answer one question from each person who passes by. And that's two."

Petronella's kind heart was touched. "Is there anything I can do to help you?" she asked.

The old man sprang to his feet. The dust fell from him in clouds.

"You have already done so," he said. "For that question is the one that releases me. I have sat here for sixty-two years waiting for someone to ask me that." He snapped his fingers with joy. "In return, I will tell you anything you wish to know."

"Where can I find a prince?" Petronella said promptly.

"There is one in the house of Albion the enchanter," the old man answered.

"Ah," said Petronella, "then that is where I am going."

"In that case I will leave you," said her oldest brother. "For I am going to the castle of Blitz to see if I can find my fortune there."

"Good luck," said Prince George. "For I am going to the city of Gratz. I have a feeling my fortune is there."

They embraced her and rode away.

Petronella looked thoughtfully at the old man, who was combing spiderwebs and dust out of his beard. "May I ask you something else?" she said.

"Of course. Anything."

"Suppose I wanted to rescue that prince from the enchanter. How would I go about it? I haven't any experience in such things, you see."

The old man chewed a piece of his beard. "I do not know everything," he said, after a moment. "I know that there are three magical secrets which, if you get them from him, will help you."

"How can I get them?" asked Petronella.

"Offer to work for him. He will set you three tasks, and if you can do them, you may demand a reward for each. You must ask him for a comb for your hair, a mirror to look into, and a ring for your finger."

"And then?"

"I do not know. I only know that when you rescue the prince, you can use these things to escape from the enchanter."

"It doesn't sound easy," sighed Petronella.

"Nothing we really want is easy," said the old man. "Look at me — I have wanted my freedom, and I've had to wait sixty-two years for it."

Petronella said good-by to him. She mounted her horse and galloped along the third road.

It ended at a large house with a red roof. It was a comfortable-looking house, surrounded by gardens and stables and trees heavy with fruit.

On the lawn sat a very handsome young man with his eyes closed and his face turned to the sky.

Petronella tied her horse to the gate and walked across the lawn.

"Is this the house of Albion the enchanter?" she said.

The young man blinked up at her in surprise.

"I think so," he said. "Yes, I'm sure it is."

"And who are you?"

The young man yawned and stretched. "I am Prince Ferdinand of Firebright," he replied. "Would you mind stepping aside? I'm trying to get a suntan, and you're standing in the way."

Petronella snorted. "You don't sound like much of a prince," she said.

"That's funny," said the young man, closing his eyes. "That's what my father always says."

At that moment the door of the house opened. Out came a man dressed all in black and silver. He was tall and thin, and as sinister as a cloud full of thunder. His face was stern, but full of wisdom. Petronella knew at once that he must be the enchanter.

He bowed to her politely. "What can I do for you?"

"I wish to work for you," said Petronella boldly.

Albion nodded. "I cannot refuse you," he said. "But I warn you, it will be dangerous. Tonight I will give you a task. If you do it, I will reward you. If you fail, you must die."

Petronella glanced at the prince and sighed. "If I must, I must," she said. "Very well."

# Three Rewards for Three Tasks

That evening they all had dinner together in the enchanter's cozy kitchen. Then Albion took Petronella out to a stone building and unbolted its door. Inside were seven huge black dogs.

"You must watch my hounds all night," said he.

Petronella went in, and Albion closed and locked the door.

At once the hounds began to snarl and bark. They showed their teeth at her. But Petronella was a real princess. She plucked up her courage. Instead of backing away, she went toward the dogs. She began to speak to them in a quiet voice. They stopped snarling and sniffed at her. She patted their heads.

"I see what it is," she said. "You are lonely here. I will keep you company."

And so all night long, she sat on the floor and talked to the hounds and stroked them. They lay close to her.

In the morning, Albion came and let her out. "Ah," said he, "I see that you are brave. If you had run from the dogs, they would have torn you

to pieces. Now you may ask for what you want."

"I want a comb for my hair," said Petronella.

The enchanter gave her a comb carved from a piece of black wood.

Prince Ferdinand was sunning himself and working at a crossword puzzle. Petronella said to him in a low voice, "I am doing this for you."

"That's nice," said the prince. "What's 'selfish' in nine letters?"

"You are," snapped Petronella. She went to the enchanter. "I will work for you once more," she said.

That night Albion led her to a stable. Inside were seven huge horses.

"Tonight," he said, "you must watch my horses."

He went out and locked the door. At once the horses began to rear and neigh. They pawed at her with their iron hoofs.

But Petronella was a real princess. She looked closely at them and saw that their coats were rough and their manes and tails full of burrs.

"I see what it is," she said. "You are hungry and dirty."

She brought them as much hay as they could eat and began to brush them. All night long, she fed them and groomed them, and they stood quietly in their stalls.

In the morning, Albion let her out. He looked at her with admiration. "You are as kind as you are brave," said he. "If you had run from them, they would have trampled you under their hoofs. What will you have as a reward?"

"I want a mirror to look into," said Petronella.

The enchanter gave her a mirror made of gray silver.

She looked across the lawn at Prince Ferdinand. He was doing sitting-up exercises. He

was certainly handsome. She said to the enchanter, "I will work for you once more."

That night Albion led her to a loft above the stables. There, on perches, were seven great hawks.

"Tonight," said he, "you must watch my hawks."

As soon as Petronella was locked in, the hawks began to beat their wings and scream at her.

Petronella laughed. "That is not how birds sing," she said. "Listen."

She began to sing in a sweet voice. The hawks fell silent. All night long she sang to them, and they sat like feathered statues on their perches, listening.

In the morning, Albion said, "You are as talented as you are kind and brave. If you had run from them, they would have pecked and clawed you without mercy. What do you want now?"

"I want a ring for my finger," said Petronella.

The enchanter gave her a ring made from a single diamond.

All that day and all that night, Petronella slept, for she was very tired. But early the next morning, she crept into Prince Ferdinand's room. He was sound asleep, wearing purple pajamas.

"Wake up," whispered Petronella. "I am going to rescue you."

Ferdinand awoke and stared sleepily at her. "What time is it?"

"Never mind that. Come on!" she said.

"But I'm sleepy," Ferdinand objected. "And it's so pleasant here."

Petronella shook her head. "You're not much of a prince," she said grimly. "But you're the best I can do."

She grabbed him by the arm and dragged him out of bed and down the stairs. His horse and hers were in a separate stable, and she saddled them quickly. She gave the prince a shove, and he mounted. She jumped on her own horse, grabbed the prince's reins, and away they went like the wind.

They had not gone far when they heard a tremendous thumping. Petronella looked back. A dark cloud rose behind them, and beneath it she saw the enchanter. He was running with great strides, faster than the horses could go.

Petronella desperately pulled out her comb. "The old man said this would help me!" she said. And because she didn't know what else to do with it, she threw the comb on the ground.

Immediately a forest rose up. The trees were so thick that no one could get between them.

Away went Petronella and the prince. But the enchanter turned himself into an ax and began to chop. Right and left he chopped, the blade flashing, and the trees fell before him.

Soon he was through the wood, and once again Petronella heard his footsteps thumping behind.

She reined in the horses. She took out the mirror and threw it on the ground. At once a wide lake spread out behind them, gray and shining.

Off they went again. But the enchanter sprang

into the water, turning himself into a fish as he did so. He swam across the lake and leaped out of the water onto the other bank. Petronella heard him coming —*thump! thump!* — behind them again.

This time she threw down the ring. It didn't turn into anything, but lay shining on the ground.

The enchanter came running up. As he jumped over the ring, it opened wide and then snapped up around him. It held his arms tight to his body, in a magical grip from which he could not escape.

"Well," said Prince Ferdinand, "that's the end of him."

Petronella looked at him in annoyance. Then she looked at the enchanter, held fast in the ring.

"Bother!" she said. "I can't just leave him here. He'll starve to death."

She got off her horse and went up to him. "If I release you," she said, "will you promise to let the prince go free?"

Albion stared at her in astonishment. "Let him go free?" he said. "What are you talking about? I'm glad to get rid of him."

It was Petronella's turn to look surprised. "I

don't understand," she said. "Weren't you holding him prisoner?"

"Certainly not," said Albion. "He came to visit me for a weekend. At the end of it, he said, 'It's so pleasant here, do you mind if I stay on for another day or two?' I'm very polite and I said, 'Of course.' He stayed on, and on, and on. I didn't like to be rude to a guest, and I couldn't just kick him out. I don't know what I'd have done if you hadn't dragged him away."

"But then —" said Petronella, "but then — why did you come running after him this way?"

"I wasn't chasing *him,*" said the enchanter. "I was chasing *you.* You are just the woman I've been looking for. You are brave and kind and talented, and beautiful as well."

"Oh," said Petronella.

"I see," she said.

"Hmm," she said. "How do I get this ring off you?"

"Give me a kiss," said the enchanter.

She did so. The ring vanished from around Albion and reappeared on Petronella's finger.

"I don't know what my parents will say when I come home with you instead of a prince," she said.

"Let's go and find out, shall we?" said the enchanter cheerfully.

He mounted one horse and Petronella the other. And off they trotted, side by side, leaving Prince Ferdinand of Firebright to walk home as best he could.

## AUTHOR

Jay Williams always loved to make people laugh. As a young man, he was a comedian in vaudeville, a kind of stage show that was popular in the early 1900's. After that, he wrote many books for both adults and children. Some of his other funny stories are *The Practical Princess* and *The Wicked Tricks of Tyl Uilenspiegel*. With another writer, Raymond Abrashkin, he created the well-known Danny Dunn science-fiction series.

Besides writing, Mr. Williams enjoyed archery and collecting Asian art. He and his wife spent part of their time living in England. Mr. Williams died there in 1978.

# Keep Your Mind Sharp

Some words have only one meaning. Once you find out what the word means, you're prepared. The next time you see that word, it will mean the same thing. But not all words are like that. Some words have several different meanings. You have to decide which meaning makes sense in the context of the sentence.

Dilly and Dally don't know that. Imagine that they are talking to Johnny Colmer, the boy in "The Fastest Quitter in Town."

"On page 12 of the story, you say that Joe Gromering thinks he's so *hot*," Dilly says.

"Does he have a fever?" Dally asks.

"No," answers Johnny.

"Does he think he's spicy, like *hot* chili?" asks Dilly, looking confused.

Johnny groans. "Look at page 12," he says. "Joe thinks he's a good ball-player — not sick or spicy."

"Oh," says Dally. "On page 11 it says that your great-grandfather's eyes have become *bad*. Are they naughty? Do they misbehave?"

"No!" Johnny shouts.

Dilly gasps. "His eyes are mean? They do *bad* things?"

"Aargh!" cries Johnny. "Look at page 11 of the story, will you? It says right there that he can't see very well. His eyes are *bad* — they don't work properly."

Dilly and Dally look relieved.

"Listen," says Johnny. "Lots of words have more than one meaning. You have to pay attention when you read and use the context to help you figure out the right meaning. Keep your mind sharp."

Dilly and Dally look shocked. "You mean our heads should be pointed?" they whisper.

Some people never learn.

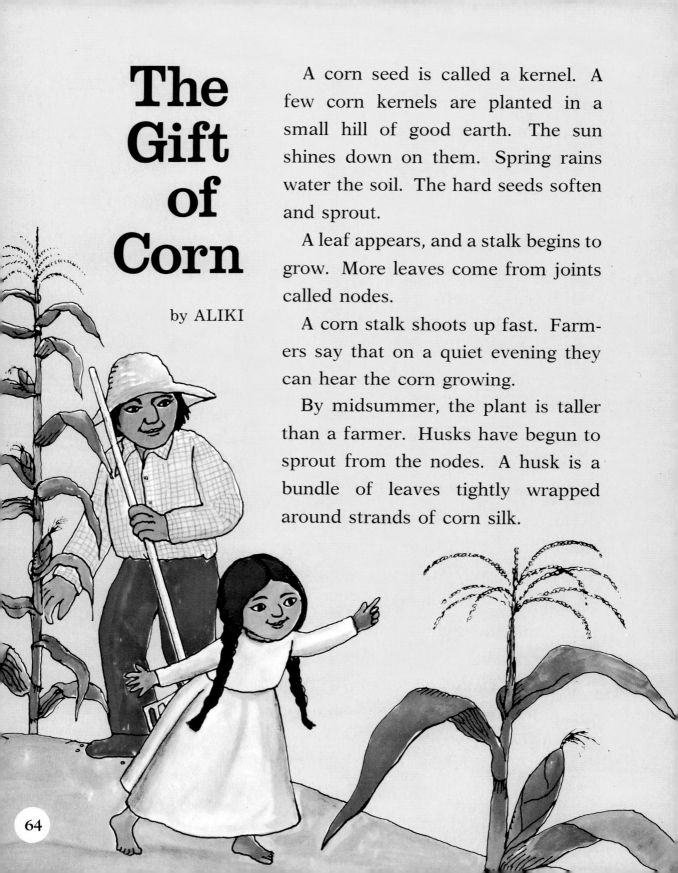

# The Gift of Corn

by ALIKI

A corn seed is called a kernel. A few corn kernels are planted in a small hill of good earth. The sun shines down on them. Spring rains water the soil. The hard seeds soften and sprout.

A leaf appears, and a stalk begins to grow. More leaves come from joints called nodes.

A corn stalk shoots up fast. Farmers say that on a quiet evening they can hear the corn growing.

By midsummer, the plant is taller than a farmer. Husks have begun to sprout from the nodes. A husk is a bundle of leaves tightly wrapped around strands of corn silk.

The corn husk grows. Inside the wrapped leaves, hundreds of kernels grow into an ear of corn.

The silk turns from a creamy color to dark red to brown. Just before it turns brown, it is time to pick the corn and husk it. The husks and the silk are pulled away.

The sweet, juicy ear of corn is ready to cook and eat.

Farmers leave some ears on the stalk. The brown silk dries. The kernels harden and are saved. They are seeds for the next crop.

Many plants can grow wild. The wind scatters their seeds over the earth, and they can grow.

Corn kernels cannot fly off the ear and scatter. If an ear fell to the ground, a sprout would grow from each kernel. The new sprouts would grow in a tangled heap and die.

So corn cannot grow by itself. Corn seeds must be planted; there must be space around each hill for the tall plants to grow. The plants must be weeded or the baby sprouts will be choked. Corn cannot grow without the help of people.

Then where did corn come from? How did it start? For many years there was no answer. It was a mystery.

Scientists know corn belongs to the same grain family as wheat, rye, oats, barley, and rice. They are all grass plants. They all have jointed stems and nodes. They all grow wild. But although scientists had searched, they had never found any wild corn.

Not long ago they found some. It was in Mexico in a cave where people once lived. They found scraps of plants and tiny ears of ancient corn, more than five thousand years old. It was not like any corn the scientists had ever seen.

At last they could piece together the story of how corn began.

In South and Central America, thousands of years ago, people lived in caves. They planted the seeds of wild grasses, perhaps those found in the caves they lived in.

Scientists think the ancient corn plant was a tall stalk with one ear at the top. Each tiny orange or brown kernel was wrapped in its own husk, or pod. The kernels grew so loosely they could fall off the cob and plant themselves.

In time, some scientists think, the pollen of other grasses helped make the corn stronger. The ears grew larger.

By the time Christopher Columbus landed in the New World, the people he named Indians were expert farmers. They harvested the corn. Some of it they ate fresh. Most of it they dried. They saved some for seed. The rest they ground into meal on a flat stone called a *metate* (may-tah'tay). They ate the meal dry or made bread with it. They cooked it into mush.

When Christopher Columbus returned to Europe, he told of the Indians and the grain they grew. He called it *maize,* which sounded like the name the Indians had used. Even today the correct word for corn is *maize*.

The word *corn* means "grain." *Corn* is the word used for the most important grain a country grows. In some countries, wheat is called corn. In others, rye is called corn. The Pilgrims called maize Indian corn, and Americans have called it corn ever since.

In parts of America, Native American farmers still grow their corn the old way. They plant the seeds as their ancestors once did. They care for the plant, harvest it, and grind it on a *metate.*

And they praise the corn that has fed their people for thousands of years.

## AUTHOR

Aliki, Mrs. Franz Brandenberg, grew up in Philadelphia, where she graduated from art school. She was first an art teacher and then an author of children's books, many of which have won awards. *Corn is Maize,* from which this article and its pictures came, won the 1976 Children's Science Book Award of the New York Academy of Sciences.

Some other books by Aliki are *Wild and Woolly Mammoths, At Mary Bloom's,* and *The Twelve Months.* She and her husband, Franz, who also writes children's books, live in New York City.

# Grandmother's Corn
by LEO POLITI

Angelica (ahn–heh′lee–kah) lived with her grandmother in the city of Pico Rivera (pee′koh ree–veh′rah) in California. The section of the city in which they lived was the "Barrio de Pico Viejo," (bah′ree–oh day pee′koh vee–ay′ho) the district of Old Pico. Many of the people who lived there were of Mexican descent.

The neighbors called Angelica's grandmother Mrs. Corrales (koh–rah′lays), but Angelica called her *Abuelita* (ah–bway–lee′tah), which means "Grandmother" in Spanish.

On weekdays Grandmother walked Angelica to school and met her for the walk home when school was over.

Angelica and her grandmother lived in an early California house with a porch all across the front. A large tree shaded the yard.

In front of the house was a vegetable garden where Grandmother grew lettuce, tomatoes, and

71

pepper plants. She also grew parsley, coriander, onions, and garlic to flavor her food. Grandmother was a very good cook, and when she was cooking, the aroma made everyone who smelled it very hungry.

At the corner of the house grew three stalks of corn. Whenever Grandmother walked by them, she stopped, caressed them, and whispered:

"*¡Qué bonito!*" (kay boh-nee'toh)

"How nice!"

Angelica asked her grandmother why she loved the plants so much. "Corn is very precious to our people," Grandmother said. "It is the basis of much of our food. No part is thrown away — even the husk is used to wrap and steam the good *tamales* (tah-mah'lays) in. And with the corn silk, we make a delicious tea."

One Saturday morning, Angelica helped her grandmother make breakfast. They decided to have buttered *tortillas* (tor-tee'yahs) and hot chocolate. Angelica made the hot chocolate. With a *molinillo* (moh-lee-nee'yoh), she whipped it to a foam. Angelica watched Grandmother very carefully as she made the *tortillas*.

First Grandmother ground the corn on a stone. The corn was soft because it had been soaked in

lime water during the night, so it quickly ground into a paste. Grandmother took a little ball of paste and patted it into the shape of a thick pancake. Angelica also took a little ball of paste, and as they patted, they hummed a song.

They placed the *tortillas* on an iron griddle to cook, and soon a pleasant odor filled the kitchen.

"Ummm!" cried Angelica as they sat at the table and ate the warm, buttered *tortillas* and drank the hot chocolate.

"When I was a little girl like you, Angelica," said Grandmother, "my mother taught me how to make *tortillas*, just as I am teaching you."

"Will you tell me more about when you were a little girl in Mexico, *Abuelita?*" asked Angelica.

"I will tell you a wonderful old legend that my mother used to tell me," her grandmother said. Angelica cuddled close as Grandmother began the story.

"Long, long ago, a great flood swept over the land. A little girl and boy climbed to the top of a mountain where they were safe from the flood waters. They were Tarahumares (tah–rah–oo–mah'rays), a people who lived and still live in that region of Mexico. When the flood waters returned to the sea, they came down from the mountain to find that they were the only survivors and that the land that had been covered by the waters was a wasteland. They had brought with

them from the mountaintop three kinds of corn — hard corn, soft corn, and yellow corn — the same varieties found in that part of the country today.

"The earth was moist and soft after the flood. The boy and girl planted the corn. Just a few days later, corn plants sprouted from the earth and grew into tall stalks. The proud plants swayed in the mountain breeze, and the golden leaves sparkled in the sunlight.

"Then they harvested the corn for food, and they lived happily there over many years. The Tarahumares believe that they are the descendants of these two survivors of the great flood."

As Grandmother finished her story, she looked out the window at the graceful corn stalks in her own yard and smiled.

One day something very special happened. The school principal came to see Angelica's teacher. He had heard that Mrs. Corrales was a wonderful cook.

"I think we should have a class where boys and girls can learn to cook good Mexican food," he said. "I have decided to ask Angelica's grandmother to teach the class."

Now Grandmother did not have to return home when she walked to school with Angelica.

At school each day, Mrs. Corrales taught the children new things. First, they learned to make *tortillas* well, because *tortillas* were the base for all the dishes they would learn to make.

In the following days, the class learned to make *tacos* (tah′kohs) and *enchiladas* (en–chee–lah′dahs). Mrs. Corrales carried to school a basket of fresh

vegetables from her garden to use in her cooking. She told the children that a *taco* is a *tortilla* filled with chopped meat, folded in half, and then fried crisp. Tomatoes, lettuce, onions, and grated cheese are then added. An *enchilada* is a *tortilla* filled with meat, cheese, or chicken, and then rolled, covered with chili sauce, sprinkled with grated cheese, and baked.

Mrs. Corrales let each child share in the cooking. One sliced the tomatoes, another grated the cheese, another shredded the lettuce. The boy who chopped the onions had tears in his eyes. Angelica, who already knew many things about cooking, helped the other children.

The children loved Mrs. Corrales's class because they found out they liked to cook, and also because at the end of the class they could eat the food they had made. There wasn't much of it because there were so many children to share it, but the little they had always tasted so good.

When Angelica and her grandmother returned home from school one day, Grandmother had a surprise for the girl. She took Angelica by the hand and led her to the dresser in her bedroom. This was where she kept her prized collection of old corn-husk dolls. Angelica loved the dolls very much.

"You have been so good and helpful, Angelica," said her grandmother, "that I am giving you all these dolls for your very own."

When Angelica went to bed that night, she could see through the window the profile of the three stalks of corn against the moonlit sky. She watched the leaves fluttering in the breeze. As she thought of all the good food and other things made of corn, she understood why Grandmother loved her corn plants so much.

## AUTHOR

The story you have just read is from the book *Three Stalks of Corn*. Leo Politi has written and illustrated many outstanding books for children. His *Song of the Swallows* won the Caldecott Medal, and he has received the Regina Medal and other honors for his work. Some of his stories have been published in Spanish.

Born in California, Mr. Politi lived for seventeen years in Italy, where he went to art school. For many years, he has lived in Los Angeles with his family and several pets.

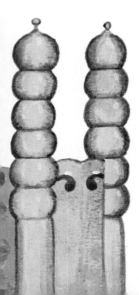

# Beauty

by E-YEH-SHURE'

This poem was written about forty years
ago by a young Native American girl.

Beauty is seen
In the sunlight,
The trees, the birds,
Corn growing and people working
Or dancing for their harvest.

Beauty is heard
In the night,
Wind sighing, rain falling,
Or a singer chanting
Anything in earnest.

Beauty is in yourself.
Good deeds, happy thoughts
That repeat themselves
In your dreams,
In your work,
And even in your rest.

# The Queen's Flowers

## by FAN KISSEN

*Cast*

| | |
|---|---|
| Queen of Sheba | Samuel |
| Amram, *a Trader* | First Man |
| Zahrah, *a Maid* | Second Man |
| King Solomon | Soldiers |
| People of the Palace | |

## Scene 1

(*The setting is a room in the palace of the **Queen of Sheba**. The **Queen** sits at one end of the room on a chair with a high back. **Zahrah** stands on one side of the chair. **Amram** is showing some silks to the **Queen**. He is standing in front of her chair.*)

**Amram:**  Would your Majesty be good enough to feel this silk?  See how fine and soft it is! (***Amram** comes a little closer to the **Queen** and holds out some purple silk.  She feels it.*)

**Queen:**  Yes, it is.  And I like this bright purple color very much.  (*She turns to **Zahrah**.*) You have a good eye for color, Zahrah.  What do you think of it?

**Zahrah:**  I like it very much, and it is a good color for a queen, your Majesty.

**Amram:**  The king of my own country, the wise King Solomon, likes this bright purple better than any other color.

**Queen:**  I'll take this purple silk, Amram.

**Amram:**  Thank you, your Majesty. (*Folds up the silk and puts it to one side.*)

**Queen:**  I have heard many things about your king.

**Amram:**  He is a good king, your Majesty, and a kind man.  All his people love him.

**Queen:**  I have heard also that he is very wise.

**Amram:**  Yes, King Solomon *is* very wise.  When his people need help, they know where to go for it.  King Solomon always has a wise word for anyone in trouble.

**Queen:** Is it true, Amram, that King Solomon understands what animals say?

**Amram:** It is true, your Majesty.

**Queen** (*Smiles*): It's very hard to believe.

**Amram:** If I told you what happened one time when I was with the king, I think you would believe it.

**Queen:** I'd like to hear your story.

**Amram:** Well, one day our king and some men of his palace were riding on horseback to a nearby city. The king was riding ahead of the rest of us. All at once he pulled his horse to a stop. He looked down at the sand in the road. The rest of us saw this happen and stopped too.

**Queen:** Go on.

**Amram:** Then the king turned his horse off the road and onto the grass. We did the same. He kept his horse on the grass a little way before turning back onto the road.

**Queen:** Did he say why he stopped and then turned his horse off the road?

**Amram:** King Solomon told us he had seen some ants hurrying along in the sand of the road. He said he had heard them say they were afraid that the horses would walk on them.

**Queen** (*Surprised*): And that was why your mighty king turned off the road?

**Amram:** Yes, your Majesty. The mighty King Solomon stopped to hear what the little ants in the sand were saying. He turned off the road to save them from being hurt.

**Queen:** Then he must be as wise and as kind as people say he is.

**Amram:** Now you can believe it, can't you?

**Queen:** I won't fully believe it until I see and hear him myself, Amram.

**Amram:** Then why don't you come to our country and pay him a visit, your Majesty?

**Queen:** Yes, I think I shall do that, Amram. But first I must think of a way to test this wise king. You may go now, Amram.

**Amram:** Good day, your Majesty. (*He backs away.*) (*Curtain*)

### Scene 2

(*The setting is a room in **King Solomon's** palace. It is a few weeks later. **King Solomon** sits in the middle of the room in a chair with a high back. There is another chair, just like his, beside him. There are windows along the wall behind the chairs. **Samuel** stands beside him, and other **People of the Palace** are standing nearby. A **Soldier** stands at the door.*)

**King** (*To Samuel*): Has everything been made ready for the visit of the Queen of Sheba?

**Samuel:** Yes, your Majesty. The best rooms in the palace are ready for her Majesty, her soldiers, and her maid.

**King:** Good! I want her visit here to be a very pleasant one.

**Samuel:** Your Majesty, I have heard that the Queen of Sheba is not coming just for a pleasant visit.

**King:** Then why is she coming?

**Samuel:** People everywhere have told her Majesty that you are a great and wise man. It is said that she is coming to find out for herself if you are really as wise as people say.

**King:** They say I am wise because I have helped them. But sometimes people in trouble cannot see how to help themselves. When I show them how to help themselves, they call me wise.

(*The sound of a trumpet is heard from outside. The* **King** *and all the others turn to the door.*)

**King:**   That must mean that the Queen of Sheba has come. Let us get ready to welcome her. (*He stands up. The others make two lines, one line on each side of his chair. The* **Soldier** *at the door calls out:*)

**Soldier:**   Her Majesty, the Queen of Sheba!

(*Two of the* **Queen's soldiers** *step into the room, followed by the* **Queen.** *She stops just inside the door.* **King Solomon** *walks over to her and bows.*)

**King:** Welcome to our country, your Majesty.

**Queen:** Thank you, King Solomon, for letting us come to visit your country.

**King:** You must be tired from your long ride. Won't you come and sit beside me?
(*King Solomon leads her to the chairs near the windows, where they sit down. The Queen's soldiers stand at the door.*)

**Queen:** Let me tell you just why I have come to visit you.

**King:** You are welcome here, no matter why you have come.

**Queen:** People everywhere have told me that you, your Majesty, are very wise. They say that you are the wisest man who ever lived. I have come to find out for myself if it is really true.

**King:** There is much that I do not know. I only try to understand my people, so that I can help them.

**Queen:** I have thought of a way for you to show me how wise you are. I have planned a test for you, your Majesty.

**King:** And what is that test?

**Queen:** First, please ask your soldier to call in my maid. She is waiting outside the door.

**King** (*Claps his hands*): Soldier! Call in the Queen's maid!

(*The **Soldier** goes out. He comes back with **Zahrah**, who holds a bunch of flowers in each hand. She walks over to the **Queen** and bows.*)

**Queen:** Give me the flowers, Zahrah. (*Zahrah hands her the flowers and moves away.*)

**King:** What lovely flowers! They all look as if they had just been picked this morning.

**Queen** (*Smiles*): Some of them *were* picked this morning. But the flowers in one bunch are not real.

**King** (*Surprised*): Not real? But they all look as if they had come from a garden.

**Queen:** One bunch was made in my country, in my own palace. Zahrah made the flowers.

**King:** I can hardly believe it! They all look so real!

**Queen:** Now I would like you to tell me, your Majesty, which flowers are real and which were made by my maid. You may look closely, but you may not touch or smell them.

**King** (*Looking from one bunch of flowers to the other*): Hm! It's very hard to tell.

**Queen:** Now we shall see if you are really as wise as people say you are!

(*She smiles, as if she has caught him in something he can't do. The* **People** *in the room look at one another and at the flowers. Then, all at once,* **King Solomon** *looks up, smiles, and claps his hands.*)

**King:** Open the windows that look out on the garden!

(**Samuel** *goes to the windows behind* **King Solomon's** *chair and opens them. Everyone looks at the windows and then back at* **King Solomon.** *The* **Queen,** *too, looks at the windows. In a few seconds, she cries out in surprise:*)

**Queen:** Look! Bees! Bees are flying in from the garden!

**First Man:**  The bees are flying to the flowers!

**Second Man:**  And they are lighting on the flowers in her Majesty's right hand!

**King**  (*Smiles, then puts his hand lightly on the flowers in the* **Queen's** *right hand*): These are the real flowers, your Majesty.

**Queen:**  You are right, King Solomon.  These *are* the real ones.

**King:**  My friends, the bees, told me.

**Samuel:** Our wise King Solomon called on the bees! He knew they could tell which flowers were real!

**Queen:** You have passed my test, King Solomon!

**King** (*Smiles*): No, your Majesty. The bees have passed your test. They are the wise ones, not I.

**Queen:** No, King Solomon. Only a wise man would have thought of letting in the bees to help him tell which were the real flowers. I have learned for myself how very wise you are. Now I can believe the stories people tell of you.

**People** (*Shout*): Long live King Solomon! Long live our wise King Solomon!

(***Curtain***)

## AUTHOR

For many years, Fan Kissen wrote children's programs for a New York radio-TV station.

Miss Kissen wrote a series of four books of radio plays. The play you have just read is from one of them, *The Golden Goose and Other Plays*. Fan Kissen died in 1978.

# The Pronunciation Key
# in a Dictionary

Most of the words that you read in stories are words that you already know. You know what the words mean, and you know how to say them.

Sometimes as you read, you come to a word that you have never seen before. You have already learned how to use a dictionary to look up the correct meaning for a word you do not know. You may also need to find out how to pronounce the word so that you can read the word aloud and use it when you talk. Besides giving you the correct meaning, a dictionary will also give you the correct pronunciation.

When you look up a word in a dictionary, you will find beside it a **special spelling** of the word. Here is the way the words *do* and *so* might look, without their meanings, in a dictionary:

**do** (do͞o)

**so** (sō)

Notice the special spelling beside each word. If you did not know how to pronounce *do* or *so,* you would have to use the special spelling and the **pronunciation key** to find out.

In most dictionaries and glossaries, the pronunciation key is at the bottom of every page or every other page. The glossary in this book uses this pronunciation key:

---

ă pat / ā pay / â care / ä father / ĕ pet / ē be / ĭ pit / ī pie / î fierce / ŏ pot / ō go
ô paw, for / oi noise / o͝o book / o͞o boot / ou out / ŭ cut / û turn / th thin / *th* this
hw which / zh pleasure / ə about, silent, pencil, lemon, circus

---

Look at the special spelling for the word *do.* The letter d in the special spelling tells you that the first sound in the word is the sound that *d* usually stands for, as in *dog* or *day.*

After d in the special spelling is o͞o. To find the sound that o͞o stands for, look at the pronunciation key. You can see that the word b**oo**t comes right after o͞o. The word b**oo**t is called a **key word.** This means that the o͞o in the special spelling stands for the

This pronunciation key is adapted from *The American Heritage School Dictionary,* copyright © 1972, 1977 by Houghton Mifflin Company.

sound for **oo** in b**oo**t. Say the word *boot* to yourself. Listen for the sound for **oo** in it. The special spelling for *do* tells you that *do* begins with the sound for *d* and ends with the sound for $\overline{oo}$.

Now look at the special spelling for the word *so*. The letter s in the special spelling shows that the word *so* begins with the sound that *s* usually stands for, as in *same* or *sand*. Look at ō in the special spelling. Now find ō in the pronunciation key. The key word right after ō is g**o**. This tells you that the sound for ō in the key word g**o** is the same as the sound for ō in the special spelling for *so*.

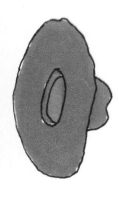

Look at the other key words listed in the pronunciation key. As you say the words to yourself, listen for the vowel sounds and the sounds for

Wō!

certain other letters in the pronunciation key. At the end of the pronunciation key is something that looks like an upside-down *e* (ə), called a **schwa.** The schwa usually occurs only in words with more than one syllable. Say the five words listed after the schwa to yourself. Listen to the sound the heavy, dark letter stands for in each word. This will give you an idea of the schwa sound.

In special spellings, you will often find one vowel standing for the sound of two vowels to-gether. For example, the special spelling for *seat* is sēt. By using the pronunciation key, you find that the *ea* in *seat* is the same sound as the ē in b**e.**

You will also find that the final *e* and some other final letters in a word may be missing from the special spelling for that word. For example, the special spelling for *kite* is kīt. The special spelling for *through* is thro͞o.

Use the special spelling and the pronunciation key to get the pronunciation for the following two words that you may not know:

**roux** (ro͞o)      **chaise** (shāz)

A special spelling will often have consonants that are different from those in the word itself. Always use the sounds for the consonants in the special spelling to learn how to say the word. Notice the special spelling for *chaise*. Think of how you usually say the letters *sh* and *z*. Then use the pronunciation key to find out the sound for ā.

When you want to find out the correct pronunciation for a word, follow these four steps:

1. Find the word in a dictionary.
2. Look at the special spelling for the word.
3. For the consonants in the special spelling, use the sounds that those consonants usually stand for.
4. For each vowel in the special spelling, look at the pronunciation key. Use the vowel sound you hear in the key word.


REVIEW

1. What two things in a dictionary tell you how to pronounce a word? Where can you find each one? How do you use them to find the correct pronunciation for a word?
2. What is the key word for the vowel sounds in *roux* and *chaise?*
3. Use the glossary at the back of this book to write the key word for the vowel sound in each of the following words:

   **hurl      scone      rein      plaque      niche**

## USING THE PRONUNCIATION KEY

The words in heavy, dark print in the story below may be new to you. See if you can get the meaning for each new word from the context. Then use the glossary at the back of this book to check on the correct meaning of the word and to find out how to pronounce the word.

Carla, Marvin, and Skip were walking past a movie theater. They saw a **queue** of people in front of the ticket window. The people were waiting to see *The Monster Who Loved to Sail Yachts.*

"My mother once sailed around the **Isle** of Pines," said Marvin.

"I **loathe** sailing," said Skip. "I always get seasick."

"Listen," said Carla, "are we going to this movie? It sounds dull for a monster movie."

"You're right," said Marvin. "Let's go see *The Eggplant That Ate New York.*"

from

# A Toad for Tuesday

by RUSSELL E. ERICKSON

TREASURE

In the middle of winter, Warton the toad decided to take some delicious beetle brittle to his Aunt Toolia. His brother, Morton, tried to talk him out of it, but Warton's mind was set. He put on his heaviest sweaters and strapped on his homemade skis. His brother packed some food for him and wished him luck.

On the way, he rescued a mouse that was half-buried in the snow. The grateful mouse gave Warton a bright red scarf. If Warton wore the scarf, the mouse said, all of the mouse's relatives would know that the toad was a friend, and they would help him if he ever got into trouble. The mouse also warned Warton about a dangerous owl who hunted by day, when other owls slept. No sooner had Warton left the mouse than he found himself being chased by this owl. In trying to escape, Warton crashed into a pile of stones, hurting his foot and losing his skis. Suddenly, he was grabbed by strong claws and lifted into the air. The owl carried Warton to his home — a hole near the top of an oak tree.

It was dark inside and smelled musty. The owl sat him in a corner and stepped back. He gave the toad a piercing look.

"What's your name?" he said.

"Warton."

"Warton?" said the owl. "Well, I think I'll call you . . . Warty."

"I don't care for that very much."

"You don't? Well, that's too bad . . . Warty!"

The little toad got up all his courage and looked right at the owl. "Are . . . are you going to eat me?"

The owl opened his yellow eyes wide. "Am I going to eat you? Of course I'm going to eat you!" Then the owl walked across the room. On the wall a large calendar hung crookedly. The owl pointed to it. "Do you know what this says?"

The toad looked at it closely. "Yes, it says BERNIE'S GARAGE — BRAKES AND FRONT ENDS OUR SPECIALTY."

"No! I don't mean that. You're not very bright, are you? It says that in five days it will be Tuesday. And next Tuesday happens to be my birthday. And finding a little toad in the middle of winter is going to make me a special birthday treat. So, until that day, Warty, you may do as you please. From the looks of your foot, I needn't worry about your trying to hop away. Besides, there is no way you can possibly get down from this tree."

The toad looked at his foot. It was twice its normal size. He gave a big sigh. Then he glanced around. . . .

"As long as I am here, I would like to make myself comfortable," said Warton. "Do you mind if I light some candles? It seems very dreary in here."

"Dreary?" said the owl. "It seems dreary? Well, go ahead if you want to. It doesn't matter to me."

The toad dug into his pack and pulled out two beeswax candles. As soon as they were lit and began casting their warm glow about the room, he felt much better. He began to straighten his corner. And, being of a cheerful nature, he began to hum a little tune.

The owl couldn't believe his ears. "Warty, you did hear me say that I was going to eat you next Tuesday, didn't you?"

"Yes," said the toad.

103

The owl shook his head.

Warton continued to busy himself in his corner. Then he turned to the owl and said, "What's your name?"

"I don't know," said the owl. "I guess I don't have one."

"What do your friends call you?"

"I don't have any friends."

"That's too bad," said Warton.

"No, it isn't too bad," snapped the owl. "Because I don't want any friends and I don't need any friends. Now, be quiet!"

Warton nodded. After a while he said, "If you did have a name, what would you like it to be?"

The owl began to be a little flustered. He wasn't used to talking to anyone, especially in his home. "Well, if I had a name . . ." he said slowly, "if I had a name . . . if I had a name, . . . I think I would like . . . George."

"Uh huh," said the toad. He went back to straightening his corner.

The owl was becoming sleepy. He fluffed his feathers and closed his eyes.

Just as he was beginning to doze off, the toad called, "Hey, George!"

The owl's eyes popped open. "Are you talking to me?"

"Yes," said the toad. "Do you mind if I make some tea?"

"Oh, go ahead," said the flabbergasted owl.

Warton took some more things out of his pack and prepared the tea. . . . Shortly, he had a steaming pot of refreshing tea.

"It's ready, George," said the toad.

"What's ready?" growled the sleepy owl.

"Our tea."

"I don't want any."

"But I've already got it poured," said Warton.

"Oh, all right," grumbled the owl.

So, by the light of the beeswax candles, the owl and the toad sat down to tea. . . .

Then the toad talked, and the owl listened. Then the owl talked, and the toad listened. It wasn't until the latest hours of the night that the owl finally said, "I'm too tired to talk any more." And he went to sleep.

Warton put away the teacups, and then he put out the beeswax candles. As he lay in the still darkness, he tried very hard to think of what he should do. But, because of the very busy day he had had and because of all the new experiences, his tired head just would not work at all. He was soon snoring softly.

When the toad awoke the next morning, the owl was gone. The swelling on Warton's foot had gone down, but it was still quite sore. . . .

Warton poked through his pack trying to find something that would be just right for breakfast. He selected an ant-egg salad sandwich. As he unwrapped it, his eyes turned to the wall opposite the doorway. A ray of sunlight fell directly on the owl's calendar. A large circle had been drawn around the day of his birthday, and an X put upon the day just past.

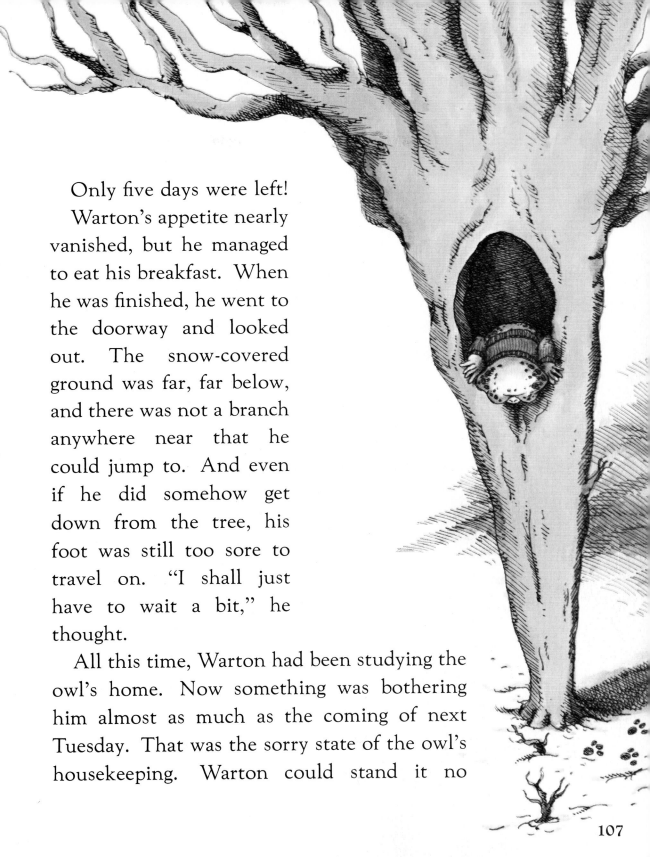

Only five days were left! Warton's appetite nearly vanished, but he managed to eat his breakfast. When he was finished, he went to the doorway and looked out. The snow-covered ground was far, far below, and there was not a branch anywhere near that he could jump to. And even if he did somehow get down from the tree, his foot was still too sore to travel on. "I shall just have to wait a bit," he thought.

All this time, Warton had been studying the owl's home. Now something was bothering him almost as much as the coming of next Tuesday. That was the sorry state of the owl's housekeeping. Warton could stand it no

The calendar reads:

BERNIE'S GARAGE - BRAKES
AND FRONT ENDS OUR SPECIALTY

| S | M | T | W | TH | F | S |
|---|---|---|---|---|---|---|
|   | 1 | 2 | ✗ | 4 | 5 | 6 |
| 7 | 8 | ⑨ | 10 | 11 | 12 | 13 |
| 14 | 15 | 16 | 17 | 18 | 19 | 20 |
| 21 | 22 | 23 | 24 | 25 | 26 | 27 |
| 28 | 29 | 30 | 31 |   |   |   |

longer. Immediately he set about cleaning up the mess. . . .

All morning and all afternoon he cleaned. He didn't even stop for lunch. He had barely finished his work when he heard the soft flapping of wings.

The owl had returned a little earlier than usual. He had never thought of cleaning his home, so he was astonished at what he saw.

"It doesn't look too bad, Warty," he said. Then he puffed himself up, and his eyes opened wide. "But don't think I'm going to change my mind about next Tuesday."

"I didn't do it for that reason," said Warton. He went to his pack, . . . unwrapped another of the sandwiches Morton had made for him, and quietly ate his supper. . . .

When Warton swallowed the very last bite, the owl said, "Are you going to make tea again tonight?"

"Perhaps I will," said Warton.

"Perhaps I will have some too," said the owl softly.

So that night the toad and the owl once again sat down to tea. And once again it was very late before they went to sleep.

The following morning, when the toad awoke, the owl was gone as before. Warton's foot felt much better, so the first thing he did was to look at the calendar. "Only four more days — I must do something soon," he thought anxiously.

He went to the doorway and looked down — it was still just as far to the bottom of the tree. . . .

He decided to clean the owl's home again. When there was nothing left to clean, he ate his lunch. Then he did some jumping exercises to clear his head for serious thinking. When his head was clear, he squatted under the kitchen table and began to think.

First one eye blinked, then the other. Slowly, at first, then faster and faster he blinked, until everything became a blur. Then he stopped, smiling.

He hopped to the doorway again and looked down. "I think two and a half will do it," he said, hopping back to his corner. Opening his pack, he took out his three tightly-knitted sweaters — the blue one, the yellow one, and the white one with the red reindeer.

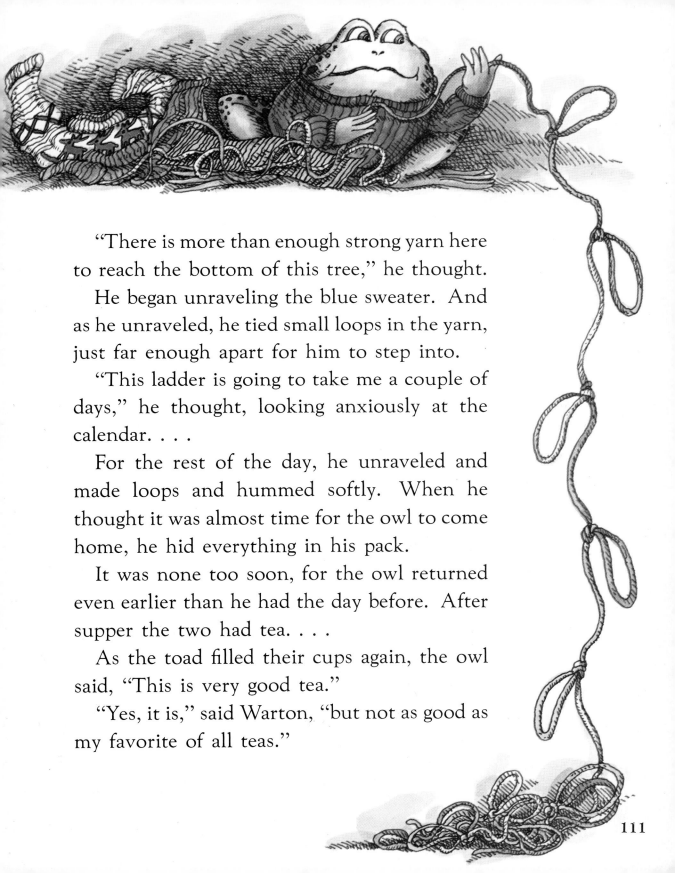

"There is more than enough strong yarn here to reach the bottom of this tree," he thought.

He began unraveling the blue sweater. And as he unraveled, he tied small loops in the yarn, just far enough apart for him to step into.

"This ladder is going to take me a couple of days," he thought, looking anxiously at the calendar. . . .

For the rest of the day, he unraveled and made loops and hummed softly. When he thought it was almost time for the owl to come home, he hid everything in his pack.

It was none too soon, for the owl returned even earlier than he had the day before. After supper the two had tea. . . .

As the toad filled their cups again, the owl said, "This is very good tea."

"Yes, it is," said Warton, "but not as good as my favorite of all teas."

"What is that?" asked the owl.

"Juniper-berry tea. My cousin once brought me some. I've never tasted any as good. But it grows only in certain places, and I've never had it again."

And they talked some more.

After Warton blew out the beeswax candles he said, "Goodnight, George."

There was a long, long silence. Then the owl said, "Goodnight, Warty."

The next day was just the same. In the morning when the toad awoke, the owl was gone. Warton worked on his unraveled-sweater-ladder until the owl returned. Later, they drank some tea and had a chat.

On Sunday morning, even though his ladder wasn't finished, Warton decided to test it. He fastened one end to the owl's saggy sofa. The other end he dropped out of the doorway. Lying on his belly, he placed one foot over the edge and into the first loop. That one held. . . .

But Warton had to be sure that his ladder would really work. So down he went to another loop, another, and then another. Finally he was satisfied.

Climbing back up was much more difficult. Warton was all out of breath when he crawled into the owl's home. . . .

As he put the ladder in his pack, a thought came to him, "Maybe George will change his mind. Then I won't need this ladder at all." Warton was thinking about how the owl came home earlier and earlier each day and how he seemed to enjoy their chats very much. At times he even seemed almost friendly. "Why, he may not eat me after all!" The thought suddenly made Warton feel quite happy.

But that day, the owl returned home later than he had ever done before. It was almost dark when he stepped through the doorway.

Warton was still feeling quite happy. "Good evening, George," he said cheerily. "Did you have a nice day today?"

The owl stood staring down at the toad, his eyes cold as ice.

"No . . ." he said slowly, "I did not have a nice day. . . ."

Warton's happiness vanished instantly. He knew now that to depend upon the owl's having a change of heart could be a fatal mistake. The ladder was his only hope, and yet there was so much more work to do and — the toad sighed — so little time. . . .

Then the worst thing happened: The owl discovered Warton's ladder and threw it away. He was very angry and wouldn't speak to the toad all evening. The next morning, on Warton's last day, the owl left as usual. Soon after, the toad heard a strange scratching sound that kept getting louder and louder. A hole suddenly appeared in the wall, and a mouse climbed into the room. He said his name was Sy. He had seen Warton's red scarf, and he and his family had decided to rescue the toad. Warton quickly packed and followed Sy through a tunnel that led outside. There he saw one hundred mice on skis. The mice had made them after seeing Warton ski. Forming two lines, Warton and the mice set out for Aunt Toolia's.

After a while, they stopped to rest in an open meadow. Something caught Warton's eye.

Down below, near the stream, some kind of a struggle was going on. Puffs of snow flew in every direction. Even from such a distance, a great deal of screeching and growling could be heard. When the snow cleared away for an instant, Warton saw someone he thought he knew.

"George?" he said under his breath. Shading his eyes from the bright sun, he looked again.

He was right. George the owl was struggling frantically to free himself from the jaws of a snarling fox. Warton could see at once that George didn't have the slimmest chance. Even now, the owl's wings were flapping weakly against the snow, while flying feathers filled the air.

Warton hopped to his feet and strapped on his skis.

"Where are you going?" asked Sy.

"I'm going to help George."

"George? Who's George?"

"George, the owl," said Warton.

"But . . . but . . . I thought we were helping you to get away from the owl," said Sy in bewilderment.

"Yes," said Warton, "but I just can't stand here and watch that fox eat him."

"But, he was going to eat *you*."

Warton wasn't listening. He pushed off toward the icy stream.

Sy scratched his head. "I never did understand toads. Well, come on, everyone!" he squeaked with a twitch of his whiskers. "Let's give him a hand."

At once, all the mice jumped onto their skis and pushed off after Warton. The sunny hillside was one great wave of skiing mice as they flashed over the glistening snow. A powdery cloud rose high behind them as the one hundred mice and one toad swept downwards.

The fox looked up and blinked unbelievingly. Faster and faster they came, the sharp points of their poles glittering like diamonds and each one pointing straight at him. Quickly the fox decided that he wanted no part of whatever it was.

He released the owl and bounded off through the deep snow as fast as his shaking legs would go. . . .

Warton looked sideways at the crumpled
owl. Feathers were scattered all over the snow.
Some floated slowly away in the icy stream.
The owl's wings were badly tattered, and one of
his big yellow eyes was swollen completely
shut.

As he looked at the once proud bird, Warton
felt sad.

"Hello, Warty," said the owl weakly.

"Hello, George," said the toad.

"What are you doing here?" asked the owl.

"I'm escaping."

The owl's one good eye opened wide. "Escaping? Escaping from what?" he said, clearly annoyed.

"From you," said the toad. "Today is your birthday, and you said you were going to eat me. I was to be your special treat."

The owl started to shake his head, but it hurt too much. "Didn't you see my note?" he said, sounding more and more exasperated.

"No. I — I was in such a hurry to leave."

"Well, if you had, you would have known that I was coming home soon, and that I was going to bring a surprise."

"A surprise?" said Warton.

"That's what I said. I first came here to the stream to get a nice fish for supper, which I did. But the surprise is over there, and that's where the fox caught me." The owl turned and pointed to some bluish-green bushes.

"Why, those are juniper bushes," said the toad.

"That's right," said the owl. "You said juniper berries made your favorite kind of tea, didn't you?"

Warton hardly knew what to say. "But I don't understand. . . . Do you mean you came here to pick them for me, and you weren't going to eat me, ever?"

"Of course I was going to eat you — until last night, that is." The owl spoke more softly. "Because we weren't speaking, I thought quite a bit last night. I thought about our chats and other things, and I thought that perhaps having a friend might not be too bad. I mean . . . I don't need any friends, of course, . . . but . . . if I ever do have a friend, . . . I hope he is just like you . . . Warton. . . ."

The toad hopped around to where he could look up at him. "I would be happy to be your friend, George."

The owl looked down, and a big smile slowly spread across his battered face. "Well, that's fine. That's just fine. I'm so happy I promise

120

I'll never eat another toad again." He looked around at Sy and his family. "Or a mouse, for that matter."

The mice cheered.

"Now, if I can still fly," he said, shaking out a few more loose feathers, "I'd be glad to take you the rest of the way to your Aunt Toolia's."

The toad hopped onto his back, shouting good-by and thank you to Sy and to all his family. It took the owl some time to lift out of the snow, but finally he rose into the air. The higher he flew, the stronger he became. Warton waved to the mice as, far below, they grew smaller and smaller. Then the forest trees seemed to float beneath them as they made a great circle in the blue sky and turned toward Aunt Toolia's.

# AUTHOR

Russell Erickson lives with his wife and their dog, an English setter, in Bristol, Connecticut. Some of his neighbors are toads, mice, owls, moles, and the other little animals and birds that appear in his stories. He has been a lithographer, or printer, as well as a writer. Among his hobbies are photography, skiing, and fishing — all of which show the same love of the out-of-doors that is in all his books. He also enjoys carpentry and puttering around his yard and vegetable garden.

*A Toad for Tuesday* is the first book the author wrote about the two toad brothers, Warton and Morton. This book was honored by the American Library Association as a Notable Children's Book in 1975, and it was chosen as an outstanding book by the Child Study Association. Mr. Erickson went on to write more adventures of the funny pair, including *Warton and Morton, Warton's Christmas Eve Adventure,* and *Warton and the King of the Skies.*

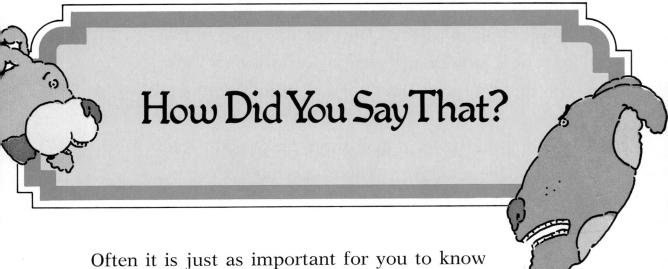

# How Did You Say That?

Often it is just as important for you to know how a character says something as it is to know what the character says. The way in which someone says something can tell you a lot about that character.

Turn to page 104 in "A Toad for Tuesday." Warton had said he felt sorry for the owl because he had no friends. But the owl made it clear that he wasn't pitiful. How? He *snapped* his reply. The author could have written, "'No, it isn't too bad,' *said* the owl." The word *snapped* helps you to know how the owl felt — proud and a bit insulted by the toad's pity.

Look at page 105. After Warton told George that tea was ready, how did the sleepy owl answer the toad? Yes, he *growled*. The owl is rather a cranky character. The word *growled* fits him.

Finally the owl agreed to have tea and answered, "Oh, all right." These words could mean just about anything, depending on how they were spoken. In the story, the owl *grumbled* them because he was not pleased to have tea with Warton. But what if the owl were looking forward to the tea party? Then the sentence might read, "'Oh, all right,' *laughed* the owl." You can see that the meaning of what was said has been completely changed.

Now, here's a game you might enjoy:

There was a knock at Maria's door. Opening it, she found Max, the joker, wearing a mask.

Maria could *say* the same thing and yet be reacting in a number of ways. Here are three:

1. "Oh, it's you!" Maria laughed.
2. "Oh, it's you!" Maria groaned.
3. "Oh, it's you!" Maria screamed.

See if you can match each of Maria's reactions with one of the following statements:

A. Maria was frightened by Max's jokes.
B. Maria loved Max's jokes.
C. Maria thought Max's jokes were boring.

# Books to Enjoy

**Cranberry Mystery** by Wende and Harry Devlin
Maggie and Mr. Whiskers help to clear up the mystery of the disappearances in Cranberryport.

**How Far, Felipe?** by Genevieve Gray
In 1775, a boy and his burro, traveling with a group of Mexican settlers, have a hard journey to California.

**Carrie's Gift** by Efner Tudor Holmes
Carrie becomes friendly with the lonely old man who saves her dog.

**The Easy Baseball Book** by Jonah Kalb
You can learn how to play better baseball with these easy-to-read, easy-to-follow directions.

**Magic in the Mist** by Margaret Mary Kimmel
On a misty day, a young boy meets a very helpful little dragon.

**Half a Kingdom** by Ann McGovern
In this unusual folktale from Iceland, a poor girl rescues a prince and wins half a kingdom.

# Weavers

MAGAZINE TWO

# Contents

# All Except Sammy

by GLADYS YESSAYAN CRETAN

Everyone in Sammy Agabashian's family was musical — except Sammy.

Mama played the piano.

Brother Armen played the clarinet.

Sister Lucy played the cello.

Papa played the violin and was the conductor of a whole symphony orchestra.

Sammy played baseball.

Sometimes the family gave a concert together. They played many kinds of music — sonatas and mazurkas and waltzes. Usually Papa and Armen did a duet especially written for violin and clarinet. Mama and Lucy always looked beautiful up on the stage in their long silk dresses.

Sammy sat in the audience and listened with the others.

---

Adapted from *All Except Sammy* by Gladys Yessayan Cretan. Published by Little, Brown and Company.

When Armen played in his own recitals, or Lucy in hers, Sammy sat in front and clapped proudly along with Papa. Sometimes people around them shouted "Bravo!" and then Mama smiled happily.

Everyone said, "Such a talented family. All so musical."

Of course they meant everyone was talented but Sammy.

One day a man from the newspaper came to take a picture of these musical Agabashians. He grouped them all around the piano. Mama sat at the piano bench, with her music spread in front of her. Armen stood next to her with his clarinet, ready to play. Lucy sat with her cello, and Papa was a little to the side with his baton raised.

Then the reporter turned to Sammy. "And what do you play?" he asked.

"Baseball," said Sammy.

"That's a good game, but I can't put you in this picture," said the man. "This is a picture of a musical family."

So, while the picture was taken, Sammy sat and watched.

Afterward, he said to his mother, "I sure would like to be in the next family picture. What instrument could I learn?"

"We could use another violinist," his mother said. "We'll ask Papa to give you lessons."

Papa tried.

And Sammy tried.

But it never did sound right. In fact, it sounded horrible. When Sammy was playing, the cat scratched on the door to be let out, and

the dog hid under the bed and howled. Even Sammy's best friend, Jason, quietly rolled his eyes and went home.

"Sammy," said his father, "even for a beginner, this is terrible."

"Let's try the piano," said his mother, "and work on your rhythm."

For days and days they worked, and Sammy tried hard.

"Oh dear," said his sister, Lucy.

"Something's wrong," said his brother, Armen.

"*Hereek!* Enough!" said his father. "Mama, the boy has no rhythm. Absolutely no rhythm."

"Try again, Sammy," said his mother. "Listen now. One-and-two-and — no, no, no, Sammy. Can't you hear the beat?"

She sat back and shook her head. *"Vagh!"* she said. "I'm afraid your father is right."

Then she had another thought. "Perhaps he will be our singer. And someday he will sing arias. Come, Sammy, what would you like to sing?"

"Take Me Out to the Ball Game," said Sammy happily.

"All right," said his mother, and she started to play it on the piano. "Come," she said. "Sing out, Sammy."

And Sammy tried. He knew all the words. He sang the very best he could, and loud.

They all listened. And they all shook their heads.

"Tone-deaf," said his father. "He can't sing a note."

"How can this happen in this family?" said his mother. "Can the fruit fall so far from the tree?"

"Mama," said his father, "stop trying. It is like baking a stone. Nothing will come of it."

"Don't feel bad, Sammy," said his sister. "It doesn't matter."

"Who's feeling bad?" said Sammy.

"Come on," said his brother. "Let's go out and play ball."

"Who cares about music anyway?" said Sammy. But Sammy really did want to be in a family picture.

After school the next day, Sammy dashed home and ran upstairs to get his bat and mitt.

"There is a thunder in our house," said his mother.

"A thunder called Sammy," said his father as Sammy rumbled down the stairs. "And look at that black cloud on his face. Why do you frown?"

"You'd frown too," said Sammy, "if you had to go to the museum."

"No," said his mother. "I often go, and it makes me happy. But why do you suddenly want to go to the museum?"

"Who wants to go?" said Sammy. "It's our homework. This week everybody has to go to the museum and find a favorite picture and tell about it."

"A good idea," said Papa.

"Listen," said Sammy. "I don't know anything about paintings. I don't even like them. How can I have a favorite?"

"Try," said his mother. "Slow down once and really look."

"One question," said his father. "Why the baseball bat?"

"Well," said Sammy, "I can't stay all day at the museum. I have baseball practice. And we're up for the championship."

He walked slowly to the museum, hitting each telephone pole with his bat. At the big gray building he stopped and wondered.

He hadn't ever gone in before.

He walked up the wide stone steps, and when he came to the great doorway, he stopped again. He felt small.

When he stepped into the large center room with its statues and its curving stairs and its cool marble walls, he looked around slowly.

His footsteps were very loud. A museum guard came up to him and told him he would have to check his bat at the front desk.

Then he climbed the stairs and wandered through the bright rooms. There were paintings of sunflowers, of children dressed in blue velvet, of dancers, pink on white.

Sammy shrugged and gave his mitt a punch. "Too fancy," he said.

He passed a picture of an old castle, of a golden-haired family, of a bowl of fruit shining in the sunlight. He shook his head.

When he saw a sparkling picture of small boats sailing, he paused. That was better. But after a moment, he walked on, wondering if he ever would find a real favorite.

He came back up the stairs, and that was
when he saw the painting of a brilliantly
dressed soldier sitting tall on a proud black
horse.

"There!" he said. "There's a picture I could
talk about." And he stopped and looked at it
for a long time.

Across the quietness a voice said, "Hi,
Sammy!" Sammy turned to see his friend Jason
standing in front of a large picture of the sea.

"Hi!" said Sammy. "Find your picture?"

"I guess I like this one," said Jason. "Looks
like a big storm. What about you?"

"I'll tell about this one," Sammy said. "But we'd better go now. We're late, and they can't start the game without us."

The next day Sammy told his class about the picture.

"And that horse could gallop or trot or run like the wind," Sammy said. Jason looked puzzled.

"Say!" he said later. "How could you tell how that horse could run?"

"You could see it in the picture!" said Sammy.

"Now look," said Jason. "I saw that picture, and I didn't see anything like that. And you even said that he had led a parade!"

"I could tell that partly from the ornaments he was wearing and partly from the proud way he held his head," Sammy answered. "Listen, if you don't believe me, we'll stop there today on the way to the ball park and I'll show you."

"All right," said Jason. "But man!" He rolled his eyes. "Gallop and trot?"

"Look," said Sammy after school as they stood in front of the picture. "Look at the power in that horse. Look at his smooth muscles. You mean to tell me that horse can't run? And see how the soldier is holding the reins. He's sure of that horse. He knows he can do anything!"

After a long look, Jason shook his head. "That's a lot to tell from a painting," he said.

Sammy nodded. "It's a lot for someone to show, just with a little paint," he said.

Jason moved slowly on around the large room. But Sammy sat on a bench and kept looking at the same picture. Jason tried walking in a circle on his heels. He swung his mitt around and around and went downstairs for a drink of water. He whistled between his teeth. When he came back, Sammy still wasn't ready to go.

Jason scuffled his feet and waited and waited. "Didn't you see enough?" he asked at last.

"Look at this," Sammy answered.

"Same old picture," said Jason.

"I've been looking at the soldier's cape," said Sammy. "It's supposed to be red."

"Sure is red," Jason said. "Bright red."

"Yes," said Sammy. "When I first saw it, I thought it was plain red. But I've really been looking at it. And I see that when you're close to it, part of it is orange, part of it is almost black, and part of it is white. But when you back away from it, it all comes out red."

Jason nodded. "I suppose an artist knows how to do that," he said.

"I'd like to know how to do it too," Sammy said. "Look how he used the white and the dark to make it look like folds in the cape. Listen, that's harder to figure out than any puzzle. I'll have to come back tomorrow and look at that some more."

Jason groaned. "More?" he said.

But Sammy wasn't listening. He was pointing to a sign. It said there was a painting class for school children on Saturday mornings.

"Look!" Sammy said. "That's for me."

"Good," said Jason. "Then you can learn all about that red. I sure was getting tired of studying it!"

## Just As Tough As Playing Baseball

They walked down the wide steps and turned toward the ball field, and Jason thought of something else.

"Hey!" he said. "Sammy! What about Saturday practice?"

"I'll only be a little late," Sammy said. "I wouldn't miss that."

"Sure," said Jason. "But what about Tug Smith?"

"Look," said Sammy. "We decided in the tryouts. I'm first base, and he's my substitute."

"I know," said Jason. "But if you don't come on Saturdays, . . . Oh, oh, look. He's already standing there as if he owns first base."

Across the field, they could see Tug standing with one foot on either side of first base. When he saw them cutting across the field, he folded his arms and pulled himself up tall.

"He's not planning to move," said Jason.

"Too bad," said Sammy. "Hi, Tug."

"Hi," said Tug. "They need someone in left field."

"Good," said Sammy. "Then you can still play."

"Not me," said Tug. "I'm first base."

"Since when?" said Sammy.

"Since you were late twice in a row."

"Listen," said Sammy. "I have to be late every Saturday, and you're my sub, fair enough. But I was chosen first base, and I'll be here as fast as I can."

"How come you'll be late?" asked Tug.

Sammy hesitated. "I have to take a class."

"No school on Saturday," said Tug.

"I know," Sammy said. "This is a special class. Art. At the museum."

"Art?" hooted Tug. "Art? Hooo-eeee! Hey, fellas, he's going to be a painter."

"Listen," Sammy said. "You're so smart. Can you paint a brown-black horse that looks like he can really run?"

Tug shook his head.

"Okay, and can you paint a storm at sea, or can you use orange and gray and white and still have a cape look red?"

"No," said Tug.

"Neither can I," said Sammy. "But that's what I'm going to try to learn. And it's tough. Just as tough as playing baseball. See?"

Tug nodded and Sammy continued, "So I'll be a little late on Saturdays, and you can sub. Right?"

"Well," said Tug. He looked down at first base. Then he looked at all the faces around him, and back to Sammy. "Well, all right," he said.

So every Saturday while Mama gave piano lessons downstairs and Armen and Lucy practiced their instruments upstairs and Papa went to symphony practice, Sammy went to the art class.

"What about the baseball team?" Papa asked as he walked one morning with Sammy toward the museum.

"I get there a little late," Sammy said. "But the fellows don't mind because I'm painting a poster for them. We'll be the only team with our own special colors and our own poster to put up whenever we're playing."

"They're lucky to have an artist on the team," said Papa. "Look at the trouble we have getting our program covers designed. And our posters for the front of the concert hall. *Agh!* Either they look like a grocery list or they look like circus posters! A musician needs a musical poster. Ah, well. Here's the museum. Learn well!"

When Jason arrived later, Sammy was sitting quietly in front of a picture of a little girl, looking, looking.

"Studying something new?" asked Jason.

"Blue," said Sammy. "This week I'm studying blue for a new painting I started. Look." He pointed. "Look at that blue dress. Part green and part black, but it all comes out blue."

"That's a fact," said Jason. "Never saw it that way before." He picked up Sammy's mitt and gave it a punch. "We get to use the big field today," he said. "Can you play late?"

"Sure," said Sammy. "There's no use going home early today, anyway. There's a man coming to our house to take a picture of the family."

"You're in the family," said Jason.

"I know," said Sammy. "But he only wants the musicians in the family. All but me."

"Never mind, Sammy," said Jason. "Maybe you can't fiddle, but you sure can draw."

"That's true," said Sammy. "I can draw. And I've been thinking. Why can't I design the program cover for their concert? And I'll bet I could plan a good poster. I could paint the instruments that they play . . . maybe in blue like in this picture. . . ."

Sammy worked hard. He worked for days and days. Sometimes he painted at the museum and sometimes at home. While he worked he would hum, "Take me out to the ball game. . . ."

"*Vagh,*" said Mama under her breath when she heard him.

"Tone-deaf," said Papa, shaking his head.

But one day Armen called, "Look! Look at Sammy's poster!"

And Lucy said, "Why, this is better than any poster we've ever had."

And it was.

So this time when the reporter came, he put Sammy right in the middle of the family, holding his poster. And when the picture of all the Agabashians appeared in the newspaper, they were called "An Artistic Family."

"Boy!" said Sammy. "Look at that! I finally got in the picture."

"And why not?" said his father. "Must everyone play an instrument? No. You are an artist. And a good one!"

"Not only that," said Armen, "he's a good ballplayer."

"Championship game tomorrow," said Lucy.

"We'll be there," said Papa Agabashian. "All of us."

And the next day, there they were, sitting on the bleachers, cheering the team. There were all the talented Agabashians — except Sammy.

Sammy was at home plate, swinging his bat, waiting for the pitch. When he felt the crack of his bat against the ball, he ran, ran, safe to first base!

He heard the yells and the whistles of the crowd. He heard the clapping and shouting of Jason and the team. He heard his family calling, "Bravo!"

"Sounds like music to me!" he said.

## AUTHOR

*All Except Sammy* was a natural story for Gladys Yessayan Cretan to write, since she herself is Armenian. Her parents came to the United States from Armenia when they were young.

Among Mrs. Cretan's other books are *Sunday for Sona,* which also has an Armenian background; *Lobo; Messy Sally;* and *A Hole, a Box, and a Stick.*

Mrs. Cretan and her husband live in San Mateo, California, and have two sons who are both interested in music.

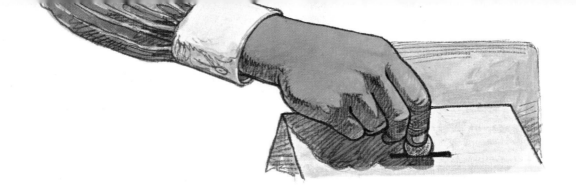

# Penny Savings Bank

by RUTH MORRIS GRAHAM

A kerosene lamp glowed on the kitchen table of a Richmond, Virginia, house in 1910. A woman sat at the table with a pair of scissors in one hand and a sheet of cardboard in the other. The only sound was the soft creak of scissors cutting through cardboard.

"No, that's not right," the woman said to herself.

"What's not right, Mamma?" asked an eight-year-old boy as he came through the door. "Are you cutting out paper dolls?"

"Well, not quite. I'm trying to make a doll house, or rather, a doll bank. Look at this, Melvin."

Maggie Lena Walker drew her son to her and showed him the lines she had drawn. Some, she said, were for cutting, and some were for folding.

"My mistake was that I was cutting a fold line. Now see, if we fold this up here, and bring that over here, these two edges will come together for pasting."

"Let me help," Melvin said. He opened the jar of paste, and trying to do as his mother told him, he smeared the edges in the right places. Some paste got in the wrong places as well, and even more paste got on his fingers.

"Oh, it's a house!" he exclaimed when his mother finished putting together the little cardboard building.

"Right. Now we'll put some words on it." Mrs. Walker picked up her pencil and began to write in large letters, P-E-N-N ——

"I see," said Melvin. "It's a little Penny Savings Bank, just like the big bank you own on Clay Street."

Mrs. Walker nodded and finished her printing. "And here on top is the slot where pennies can be dropped in," she said. "I hope this will help children learn to save."

Melvin did not understand. A penny was such a little bit of money, and all around him he heard adults talk about dollars.

"But why should children save pennies?" he asked.

"Saving is important," his mother said. "It's more important for poor people than for rich ones. You know, we would not have the bank if a lot of black people hadn't saved their money. And most of us started by saving pennies."

"But you never had to save pennies. You're rich."

"Melvin, when I was your age, I was very poor. My parents were poor."

"Were you a slave?" the boy asked.

"No, but your grandmother and grandfather were. I was born *after* the Civil War. Still, my parents had never been to school. They couldn't earn much money. Then my father died, and my mother worked hard to raise her children and send us to school. That was when she taught us about saving, for whenever she had work, she always saved for the time when she might not. She had to save, mostly one and two pennies at a time, to get enough money to buy us clothes and to pay her bills."

Melvin looked at his mother with wide eyes. "I'm glad you're not poor now, Mamma," he said. "Now that you're president of a bank, you don't have to work hard like your mother did."

Maggie Lena Walker was also glad that she no longer was poor, but she did not feel that she was rich. Nor did she feel that she no longer had work to do. She knew that many black people were very poor and needed to learn how to save money. And with her Penny Savings Bank models, she felt she could teach them.

The next day she took her sample bank to a printer. She ordered five thousand sheets of cardboard with lines and letters like those on the sample.

The following week she started her rounds of schools. In Virginia in those days, black and white children did not go to the same schools. Mrs. Walker visited the schools in Richmond that had black students. The teachers there knew that she had founded the St. Luke Penny Savings Bank in 1903. They were glad to have her talk to the children.

In each class, Mrs. Walker talked about the bank. She told how it had opened with just the combined savings of a few people, and how it had grown as other people put in their money. In her bank, a person could start a new savings account with just one dollar.

"The many small savings accounts, added together, give the bank a large total of money," Mrs. Walker told the children. "From the large total, the bank makes loans to people so that they can buy homes, or start small businesses, or send their children away to school."

She went to the chalkboard and wrote some figures. "To make things simple, let us say that 100 savers have on deposit $10 each. This means that the bank holds 100 times $10, which equals $1,000. Let's say the bank lends $500 to a family to buy a house, $300 to a man who wants to improve his business, and $200 to some people who want to send their son to college. All the money saved by depositors in the bank will be helping these people. Do you understand that much?"

The students seemed to understand, but one boy was waving his hand. The teacher nodded to him.

"Suppose," the boy said, "that some of those depositors want to get their money back. What happens then?"

Mrs. Walker smiled. "That's a good question. Very simply, while this amount of money is being loaned out, other money is coming in. Some people are making deposits, and some people are paying back their loans. A bank never lets all its money out on loans."

Next a girl asked, "Who pays the bankers and the other people who do the work?"

"That comes from interest," Mrs. Walker said. "You see, the people who borrow money from the bank must pay interest. That is, they must pay back a little more than they borrowed. The interest is like profit for the bank. The profit from interest and from other activities enables the bank to pay its expenses and to grow."

After answering their many other questions, Mrs. Walker showed the class her model of the St. Luke Penny Savings Bank. She gave the teacher enough printed cardboard for each student to make a savings bank to take home. As soon as the boys and girls saved a dollar, the money would be sent to the real Penny Savings Bank. An account could then be opened in the name of the young saver.

This is the way the school savings-bank system was started in Richmond, Virginia. Through it, many people learned to save their money. For some, life became easier. A few became rich. And it all started with Maggie Lena Walker and her Penny Savings Bank.

## AUTHOR

After teaching school in Virginia, Ruth Morris Graham went to teach in Africa, where she wrote stories and plays for her students. While there, she met her husband, Lorenz Graham, who also writes for young people. During a family visit to the Caribbean, Mrs. Graham wrote *The Happy Sound,* a story about the island of Haiti.

# KNOWING YOUR 9'S

Do you have trouble multiplying by 9? There is an easy way to multiply 9 by any number from 1 to 10.

Let's say you want to multiply 4 × 9. Here is how you do it:

1. Hold your hands open facing you.
2. Start counting your fingers from the left until you come to the fourth finger.
3. Put that finger down.
   How many raised fingers to its left?        3
   How many raised fingers to its right?        6

So 4 × 9 = 36

Remember — count from the left until you come to the number you want to multiply by 9. Put that finger down. The raised fingers to its left stand for tens. Those to its right stand for ones.

# Pronunciation:
# Context and Stress Marks

You know that words have one or more syllables. The word *let* has just one syllable, but the
word *letter* has two syllables.

When you say a word that has more than one
syllable, you say one syllable with more stress, or
force. Say the word *begin* to yourself, and listen
to which syllable you say with more stress. It's
the second one, isn't it? Now, do the same thing
with the word *window*. In *window* you say the
first syllable with more stress.

You know how a special spelling in a dictionary
gives the pronunciation of a word with one syllable. When a word has more than one syllable, the
special spelling also shows you which part of the
word is said with greater stress.

Look at these words as they might appear,
without their meanings, in a dictionary:

> **be·gin**  (bǐ gǐn′)
>
> **win·dow**  (wǐn′dō)
>
> **eve·ry·thing**  (ĕv′rē thǐng)

A word with more than one syllable is printed with heavy dots to show you where the word is broken into syllables. Beside the word is the special spelling, which shows you how to pronounce each of those parts.

Notice the mark right after the second part of the special spelling for *begin*. That mark (') is called a **stress mark.** It shows that the part before it is said with more stress than the first part. In the word *begin,* the second syllable is said with more stress.

Now notice the stress mark after the first part in the special spelling for *window*. This means that the first syllable in *window* is said with more stress.

Look at the special spelling for *everything,* which has three syllables. Which part is said with the most stress? Yes, you know the first part is stressed because it is followed by the stress mark.

Sometimes a word may be said in different ways. It may have different meanings when different parts of the word are stressed. When that is true, you will find in the dictionary two different special spellings, each with its own meaning, for that word. You will need to read each of the

meanings to find out how the word should be pronounced.

For example, look at the following word as it might appear in a dictionary:

> **proj•ect** (**prŏj′**ĕkt) A plan, especially one that calls for careful planning and work.
>
> —**pro•ject** (prə **jĕkt′**) To shoot or throw forward.

Which meaning and pronunciation would you use for *project* in this sentence?

**I wrote a story for my class project.**

Yes, you would use the first meaning of *project,* and you would stress the first syllable of the word. The second meaning does not make much sense in the context of this sentence.

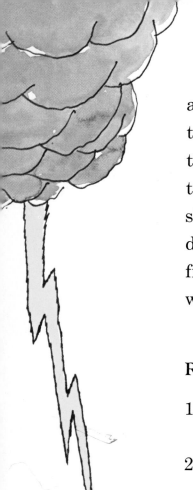

Most dictionaries have the stress mark right after the part that should be stressed. Some dictionaries, however, place the stress mark *before* the stressed part. The front of most dictionaries tells about all the marks used in that dictionary to show correct pronunciations. Before you use a dictionary for the first time, check the pages in the front of it to learn how that dictionary shows which part of a word should be stressed.

## REVIEW

1. How does a dictionary show where a word is divided into syllables?
2. How does a special spelling show which part should be stressed?

3. What should you do if you are looking up a word in a dictionary and you find two different pronunciations, each with its own meaning, for the word?

4. What two ways of showing which part to stress are used in different dictionaries? How can you find out which way is used by a certain dictionary?

5. Read the three sentences below. Copy each of the words that are in heavy, dark print, dividing it into parts and showing which syllable should be stressed. Use the context and the glossary at the back of this book to help you.

   a. The noise of the thunder was **tremendous.**

   b. The **clumsy** dog knocked over the plant.

   c. We bought a new **combine** for the farm.

## USING STRESS MARKS

Eight words in the following story are in heavy, dark print. Use the context to get the correct meaning for each of these words. Then use the glossary at the back of this book to check on the correct meaning of the word and to find out how it is pronounced. Be sure to stress the correct syllable as you say each word to yourself.

Once upon a time, a little boy named Gregory was bored. It was a **dreary,** rainy day.

"I wish I had something to do," he moaned. "I'd do almost anything to pass the time!"

Suddenly a woman appeared, wearing a long, purple dress that was beginning to **unravel** at the hem. "All right, Greg," she said. "Here's a pile of two million beads in ten different sizes. You have until tomorrow morning to **separate** them into ten different piles . . . or else!" Then she left.

The day was now a total **disaster.** Sorting two million beads into ten **separate** piles was not Gregory's idea of fun.

After three hours of work, he had to stop. His **muscles** were sore. "This is more boring than doing nothing!" he screamed. "I don't care what happens — I won't do it!"

But the next morning, Gregory found himself waiting **anxiously** for the woman's return. Suddenly she appeared. "You haven't finished, Greg," she said.

"I know," Gregory began in a **quavery** voice. "But sorting beads was so dull!"

"Well, I could have told you that," said the woman, and taking her pile of beads, she left.

# Snow

by KAZUE MIZUMURA

Please bird, don't go yet.
You are the finishing touch
To the snowy branch.


Squeals of children
Tumble down the snowy hill.
Spring is still far away.


Snow makes a new land.
One step, two steps.  I explore
The way to my school.

# Brave Janet of Reachfar

by JANE DUNCAN

Janet lived on a farm named Reachfar. It lay on top of a hill in the Highlands of Scotland and looked down toward the sea.

The nearest house to Reachfar was two miles away, but Janet never felt lonely. She had her dog, called Fly, and her family: her grandfather and grandmother, her father and mother, her aunt, and her special friends, Tom and George, who did most of the work about the farm.

Janet's grandfather was very old, with a long white beard, and he was a little deaf. Janet saw her father only in the evenings, for he managed another farm all day. Her grandmother, her mother, and Aunt Kate were always busy — especially her grandmother. Janet thought she must be the busiest woman in the whole world.

Granny was always bustling about and "laying down the law" or being "on about" things, as

George and Tom called it. Only they did not call her Granny when she was on about things — they called her Herself.

One noonday in spring, when Janet and her family were sitting at the big kitchen table having their dinner, the sun suddenly seemed to disappear and the sky went dark. Big flakes of snow began to fly past the window.

"I *told* you this was coming," Granny said, and it was in her Herself voice.

Granny always seemed to know when it was going to rain and when there was going to be a gale.

"I said it was too early in the year to put the sheep out on the High Moor and the East Hill," Herself went on. "So don't blame me now that you have to go and bring them all back into the shelter of the Home Wood again."

She spoke as if everybody was arguing with her, but nobody was saying a word. Everybody was watching the snow, which kept growing thicker and thicker. "Finish your dinner, George and Tom, and fetch the sheep back into the Home Wood."

"Yes, Granny," Tom and George said together.

They put on their heavy coats and mufflers, took their tall sticks from the rack in the hall, and called their sheepdogs, Moss and Fan, out of the barn. Then they set off toward the gate that led to the High Moor. Janet followed them with Fly, but she did not go farther than the gate. The High Moor was a forbidden place.

"We will gather the big flock off the Heights first, Tom," George said at the gate. "Those thirty ewes on the East Hill will have to wait till we get back. Run along into the house, Janet, and get out of all this snow and cold."

Janet went into the stable and climbed up to sit on the edge of Betsy's manger, while Fly lay down on a sack by the wall.

Stroking Betsy's face, Janet thought about her grandmother. She was rather beautiful, really. Her "on abouts" did not last for very long, and soon she would turn back into the person they called Granny, who was gentle and wise. She always seemed to know where you had been and what you had been up to, even when you were far away out of her sight. It seemed to Janet that Granny knew about every single thing in the whole world.

Janet gave Betsy's neck a final pat and climbed down from the manger.

She began to think of the poor sheep out on the cold East Hill. It would take George and Tom a long time to bring down the flock from the High Moor. The ewes on the East Hill would have a very long wait. . . .

Suddenly Janet buttoned up her coat and put on her woolen hood and gloves. "Heel, Fly," she said as they left the warm, steamy barn for the snow and cold out-of-doors.

The East Hill was a long way off, and today it seemed longer than ever. The wind kept trying to blow Janet and Fly backward as they plodded through the deepening snow on the path through the wood. At last, though, they came to the little gate that led out onto the bare hill where the snow was like a thick cloud of feathers.

When Janet took off her glove to undo the latch of the gate, her fingers went stiff with the cold. The East Hill was a forbidden place, too — but Janet did not intend to go right out on to it, not *right* out *on* to it.

"Seek, Fly!" she said, waving her arm at the hill, just like Tom or George. "Sheep! Go seek!"

The dog crouched low, so that her dark furry body seemed to slide under the blowing snow. She ran out onto the hill, while Janet waited in the shelter of the trees by the gate.

Soon the sheep began to come toward Janet. "One, two, three —— " she counted as the woolly creatures galloped one by one through the narrow gateway, baa-ing as if to say thank you for the shelter of the trees.

"Twenty-nine," Janet said when Fly came to look up at her. "One more, Fly! Go seek!"

Fly disappeared into the snow again and was gone for a long time. When she came back she brought no sheep with her. She put her paws up

to Janet's chest and then began to dance round and round, barking all the time and making bigger and bigger circles that took her farther and farther out on the hill.

She wanted Janet to follow her, but Janet was not sure about this. Besides being forbidden, the East Hill under the blowing snow was very wild, bare, and frightening. In the end, though, she decided to trust Fly, who always knew the way home. She shut the little gate and stepped out into the deep snow and driving wind.

She was completely out of breath, and her legs felt as if they were going to break with tiredness when, at last, Fly nuzzled into a mound of snow and exposed the head of a sheep.

"Baa-aa," the sheep said in a weak, tired voice as Janet and Fly began to dig the snow away. Fly dug very quickly with her forepaws, making the snow fly up in a cloud behind her. But it was Janet who found the baby lamb, quite newly born and tucked in close to its mother.

"Stop, Fly," Janet said, for she knew that if she picked up the lamb and began to walk away, the mother sheep would struggle free and follow her.

Janet unbuttoned her coat, put the lamb inside, and fastened the coat again with the lamb's head sticking out between the two top buttons. When Janet and Fly started to walk away, the mother sheep began to struggle hard, baa-ing pitifully. It seemed she could not get up.

"Dig, Fly!" Janet said, and soon they found that a piece of the wire fence was wound round and round the sheep's leg. Her struggling was only pulling it tighter, so that it was cutting the leg painfully.

Janet's hands were not strong enough to bend the wire, though she tried for some time. At last she sat down in the snow. Fly sat down, too, her head on one side, her golden eyes looking from the sheep to Janet as if to say, "What do we do now?"

Janet thought hard. Then she took off her woolen hood and untied her blue hair ribbon. Her fingers were numb as she tied the ribbon tightly to Fly's collar. Her lips were stiff with cold, too, as she said, "George and Tom, Fly! George and Tom!"

With the wind behind her now, Fly dashed away, the ends of blue ribbon streaming from her collar.

Janet tucked herself close into the woolly side of the sheep, took off her wet gloves, and put her

cold hands inside her coat to cuddle the lamb. She tried not to feel frightened.

The snow piled up around them, while the wind howled and shrieked across the hill. Janet began to feel warm, cozy, and sleepy. She did not know that this deceiving warm sleepiness sometimes causes people to snuggle down and be found long afterwards, frozen to death.

She was quite startled when she heard barking close beside her. Fly began to dig, her blue ribbon still streaming in the wind, and then Moss and Fan were there and began to dig too.

176

"Out of it! Get back, dogs!" said George's voice, and Janet found herself being lifted, shivering now, out of the snowy hole that had been so cozy and warm.

George turned her over his arm and began to pat her quite hard on the back. The shivering stopped.

"Careful!" she said, coming wide awake. "Mind my lamb, you clumsy big lump!"

"Merciful goodness," Tom said. "She has a lamb!"

"The mother sheep is hurt," Janet told them. "She has got wire ——"

"We'll soon see to that," Tom said, and with his strong fingers he began to untwist the wire that Janet had not been able to bend.

Janet was safe now from the storm, standing beside George and Tom, who always made everything safe. But she began to feel another kind of fear. She suddenly remembered that she was forbidden to come out onto the East Hill like this, and that there would be a scolding from Herself when she got home.

The mother sheep gave a loud "Baa!" and sprang to her feet. She was limping a little, but she would soon be all right. She came close to Janet to sniff at her lamb's head.

Janet looked up at George. "Herself and Mother are going to be angry," she said.

"Angry? After you bringing in the flock from the Hill and bringing home the first lamb of the spring?" George asked.

"About the East Hill, here," Janet said.

"*What* East Hill?" George asked, looking around as if he had never heard of the East Hill. "Speaking for myself, I cannot see anything through all this snow. I do not see any East Hill around here."

"Nor me either," Tom said. "And I will tell you something. We are going to be late for tea. Herself will be so angry about that, she'll have no angriness left for anything else. Come on!"

Herself looked from Tom to George, and then on to Janet with the lamb's head under her chin. This was her suspecting look — the look she wore when she suspected that Janet, George, and Tom had been up to something.

"Baa!" the little lamb said in a small voice.

"George and Tom," Herself said sternly, "take that lamb out to the fold to its mother where it belongs."

"Right away, Granny," George said.

"This very minute, Granny," Tom said.

"And you take those wet things off," she said to Janet, "and sit down at the table beside *your* mother where *you* belong."

Janet did as she was told, and Herself went on, "Sometimes I think the people of Reachfar have no sense at all, putting sheep out, taking them in, and prowling about among the snow and the cold as if they had no brains in their heads. It is a wonder that some of *them* don't get lost in the snow."

Janet's mother was very quiet and spoke always in a soft voice. "If they got lost in the snow, Granny, you would have nobody to scold. That would be terrible, wouldn't it?" she said.

Herself looked at Mother, and Janet watched her change back into Granny. Mother could always make her do this.

Granny smiled at Janet. "But you are a clever girl, finding the first lamb of the spring like that," she said. "Eat a big tea. You must be very hungry after going such a long, *long* way, all by yourself, to find that lamb."

Granny took the lid off the big black pot on the fire and stirred the supper soup. She had a funny smile on her face — a wise sort of smile that said she knew you had gone to a forbidden place but you had done it for a good reason and must be forgiven.

Janet ate a boiled egg, a scone with butter, two scones with raspberry jam, and a piece of short-bread. It was a very nice tea.

## AUTHOR

Jane Duncan, a Scottish author of many books for adults and children, was an officer in the British Air Force and a secretary before she began her writing career. She and her husband lived for ten years in Jamaica.

Her family home in the northern Highlands of Scotland is the setting for the story you have just read. Janet's adventures continue in *Janet Reachfar and the Kelpie* and *Janet Reachfar and the Chickabird,* which was written just before the author's death in 1976.

# Special Words

What language do you speak? You'll probably answer English and perhaps another language as well. However, you may speak some special languages too. Maybe you speak "baseball" or "rock-collecting." Your doctor speaks "medicine." And the cook at your favorite restaurant speaks good "food"!

All these special languages are part of your own language, of course. But each job or hobby has its own special words.

Look at the opening of "All Except Sammy" on page 130. The Agabashians are a musical family. They use the special language from the world of music to talk about their work. The Agabashians give family *concerts*, which are musical perform-

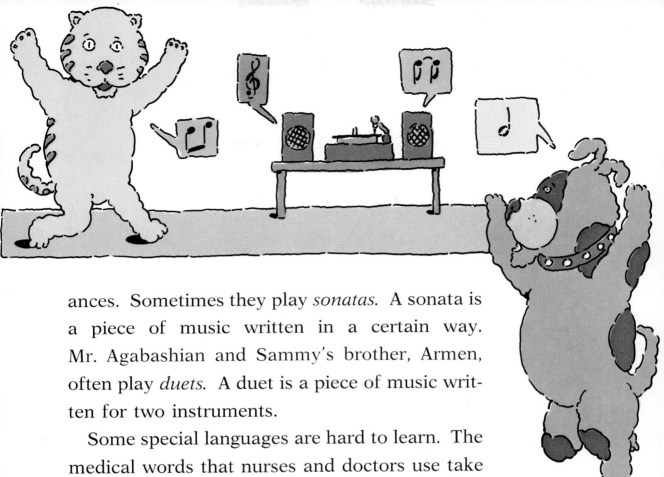

ances. Sometimes they play *sonatas*. A sonata is a piece of music written in a certain way. Mr. Agabashian and Sammy's brother, Armen, often play *duets*. A duet is a piece of music written for two instruments.

Some special languages are hard to learn. The medical words that nurses and doctors use take many years of study to learn and understand. Other jobs or hobbies use special words that are much simpler. But whether they are hard or simple, these special words do one important thing. They help people to understand one another in an exact way. That is what language is all about.

Sammy Agabashian was interested in baseball and painting. You might want to look through "All Except Sammy" again. See if you can find any special language from these two interests.

# The Great Cleanup

by N.M. BODECKER

Beetle had just moved to the quiet village of Mushroom Center. Early one summer evening, just as he was getting into bed, he heard a loud crash. Suddenly the air was filled with bangs and clangs and rattles. He ran outside, and there he found everyone else from the village looking around in amazement. Mushroom Center was a disaster area! To you, perhaps, the remains of a picnic lunch dropped somewhere in the woods doesn't mean much. But to everyone in Mushroom Center, it *was* a disaster. Mushroom houses were ruined, gardens were wrecked. They all poked around in the rubbish for a while but finally decided that the best thing to do was to get a good night's sleep. In the morning they would figure out what to do.

Early the next morning, they went to look at the damage together. Everything looked worse in daylight than it had the night before.

They found more rubbish, more candy wrappers, more crumpled tinfoil, more bits and pieces of hamburgers and hard-boiled eggs and cheese. They found a pickle stuck in Moth's chimney and an egg roll stuck in Cricket's chimney.

There were piles of tuna-fish salad and coleslaw in the Close and a chunk of knackwurst in Caterpillar's greenhouse. The thing they had heard bumping through the Fern Woods turned out to be an empty bottle, now lying peacefully in the grass.

Everywhere the mess was the same. The only new thing they found was a gob of purple chewing gum in the raspberries, and that didn't cheer them much.

Later that day, they had a town meeting at a long table under the mulberry tree in Cricket's garden. The meeting was to decide what should be done, who should do it, and how.

First they agreed to put all the rubbish together in a big pile outside of town. Spider suggested that they burn the lot. But how do you burn a tin can and a pie pan and a glass bottle?

Moth suggested that they dig a hole big enough for everything and bury it.

"That would mean a *lot* of digging. And I mean a LOT!" said Cricket. "Besides, it's such a waste — if only we could think of another way."

Then the brown beetle got up, tapped politely on his teacup with his spoon, and said that he had a plan.

This is the plan (known later as William Beetle's Garbage Emergency Plan): (1) Most of the stuff dumped on us is reusable. (2) Some is perishable and should be handled first. (3) Cut perishables into small pieces. (4) Wrap in tinfoil or candy wrapper and store them. (5) Sort out the rest of the stuff and stack for later use. (6) Repair damaged mushrooms. (7) Clean up!

"While doing this," said Beetle, "we'll have plenty of time to decide what to do with the gum, the tin can, and the rest."

When Beetle sat down, there was a burst of applause. Snail — having nothing to applaud with — said, "Bravo!" in his deep voice.

Then the meeting broke up, and they all went to work.

News of the disaster at Mushroom Center had spread throughout the woods. Friends and relatives began pouring in to ask for news and to offer their help.

Long tables had been set up on the Common. At the tables stood the townspeople and their friends and second cousins, talking as they cut and wrapped the perishables.

Moth's nieces were there, and Cricket's nephews, Ladybug's four ladylike sisters, and Spider's two spidery brothers.

Beetle had been joined by friends from the woods and the river. Caterpillar's cousins had come in great numbers to help her.

Snail's relatives, as might be expected, turned up later.

There had never been so many people in Mushroom Center, and they all worked hard.

By the end of the day, all that was perishable had been cut and sliced and scooped up and divided and cooked and bottled and wrapped and labeled and stored. Soon there wasn't a cupboard or closet or box or drawer in all of Mushroom Center that wasn't bursting with food.

The dill pickle had been cut into two thousand seven hundred and forty-nine pieces and put up in two hundred and thirty-two jars, fourteen bowls, and a jug. It had taken a gang of eleven tumblebugs (friends of Beetle) three hours and thirteen minutes to get the pickle out of Moth's chimney, using ropes and pulleys.

At the end of the second day, most of the friends and acquaintances and nearly all the relatives returned home, each carrying enough food for a month. A few stayed on, helping wherever they could.

One by one, the mushroom houses were righted and the fences mended.

One by one, the gardens were cleared, the lawns cut and raked, the lanes swept, and the hedges trimmed.

New glass was put in the windows, and new wax was put on the floors. Everything in need of a brush or sponge or rag was rubbed and scrubbed and polished. By the time they were finished, the whole village sparkled like a soap bubble.

Every day at lunch (and again after supper), they had a meeting. And at every meeting they made plans and discussed them and argued about them and turned them upside down and inside out. This, of course, is what a meeting is for.

And while they talked, Moth wrote everything down in her shadowy little hand. This is what she wrote:

*Pie Pan:* Paint blue inside, fill with water, and use as a pool. Or, paint white inside, put upside down on pieces of drinking straws, and use as a roof for an outdoor stage.

*Ice-cream sticks:* Cut into pieces — for table-tops, chests, cupboards, floors, and doors.

*Bottle:* Use, lying on its side, dug halfway into ground, and half filled with dirt, as a greenhouse. Use fireflies to light it.

*Then:* Make greenhouse and pool part of a small park.

*Also:* Pool could be used as skating rink in the winter.

They had many other ideas. Some of them Moth wrote down, and some of them she left out because — believe me — they were quite silly.

For example, Spider suggested that the straws could be cut into sections for use as barber-shop poles. No one thought much of that.

As for the purple gum, no one even wanted to think of it!

"It's strange," said Beetle, one evening when he and Cricket were sitting by the fire in his house. "That tin can, all those straws, and that mess of purple gum somehow suggest something quite simple — if only I could think of it. You do know what I mean, don't you, Cricket?"

"Oh, I do indeed!" said Cricket. But he didn't, so they talked about other things, until the fire died down and Beetle went home.

Cricket went to bed and fell asleep almost immediately. But Beetle sat down in his easy chair with a bit of paper and a pencil. Part of the night he did calculations in his head, and part of the night he wrote them down on his paper to see why they didn't come out right. Then he said, "Yes, of course ——" and "How silly of me to forget ——" until his paper was full of figures and his head was empty. Then he went to bed.

Beetle arrived a little late for their next town meeting, carrying a small bunch of papers. He put the papers on the table in front of him. When he had sorted them out, he got up to introduce his Plan for the Use of the TIN CAN, the DRINKING STRAWS, and the PURPLE CHEWING GUM. They all listened carefully.

"Place the TIN CAN on a low circular stone wall, cover with pine-needle shingles and use as a WATER TOWER. Use ice-cream sticks to build a windmill for pumping water from the spring into the tower. Use the DRINKING STRAWS to pipe water into every single mushroom house in Mushroom Center! Use the PURPLE CHEWING GUM to glue pipes together."

Along with the plan were some very wonderful little drawings of waterworks and pipes, and all kinds of facts and figures.

They elected Beetle the Waterworks Commissioner on the spot. And he accepted.

When work began the following day, some clever earthworms offered to do the plumbing. A firm of carpenter ants were in charge of the building and shingling. Caterpillars, fitted with little scoops, dug holes. Spider spun ropes for hoisting. Snail — slow but dependable — did the hoisting. Moth carried shingles to the ants. Firefly and her two younger brothers worked in the greenhouse. Ladybug set out tea, toast, and strawberry jam for everybody. And while they worked, Cricket played encouraging music for them.

When the tower was on its foundation, and the pipes were in the ground, when the pool was full of water and the greenhouse full of flowers, they put a stairway on the tower and a railing around the edge at the top. From there, a splendid view could be had of the town, the Fern Woods, the Mole Hills and — on clear days — even Robin's Rock and Turnpike's End.

Everyone celebrated that day by not having a single town meeting either before lunch or after supper. Instead, they all stayed home, turning their water taps on and off all afternoon.

Later in the week, when they were all rested, they had an evening party in the park, with speeches and balloons and colored lights in the trees. And right at midnight, the fireflies put on a display of fireworks from the top of the tower.

After that, things returned to normal. They all had their own things to look after. Some worked in their gardens. Some stacked their firewood. Some brought in their apples.

In the garden of cabbages and roses, only a single flower was left. When that died, it was summer's end. The days grew darker; the nights grew colder. The leaves came off the trees, and at last, the ground froze.

If you should ever come to that part of the woods on a snowy afternoon, look out for the Turnpike and the Common. Where they meet is the entrance to the park.

The greenhouse is lit by fireflies casting a warm glow over the rink, where the friends skate together. The snail has four skates tied on him and glides over the ice with much grace.

When they are finished skating, they all gather in the greenhouse around a teapot that never gets cold.

And there we will leave them now, under their green ferns, in the heart of winter.

## AUTHOR

Niels M. Bodecker was born in Denmark and is both an author and illustrator. After studying art, he worked for newspapers and magazines, writing and drawing cartoons. Later he came to live in the United States, where he continued to write and illustrate.

The story you have just read is from Mr. Bodecker's book *The Mushroom Center Disaster.* Another of his books, *It's Raining Said John Twaining,* which he translated for his sons from old Danish rhymes, received the Christopher book award. *Hurry, Hurry, Mary Dear!* is his third collection of nonsense poems and is also an award winner.

# Musical Pets

by LEONA MEALS

Some children have music boxes. Others keep canaries. In Japan boys and girls often keep musical insects as pets.

There are more than a dozen different kinds of singing insects, but crickets are the most common. In Japan cricket pets are kept in bamboo cages. They are easily tamed. In a few days a cricket becomes used to its new home. It will recognize its owner's voice and chirp without stopping when he or she is near. Having a cricket in the home is supposed to bring good luck. In return for its singing, the cricket is fed all the slices of fresh cucumber it can eat.

Japanese children may catch their crickets and some other singing insects in their own yards and gardens. Or if they have money to buy them, they may go to a store, just as you might to buy a pet goldfish or a pet parakeet.

You would be amazed to hear the insects' range of musical notes. *Kusahibari*, known as the grass lark,

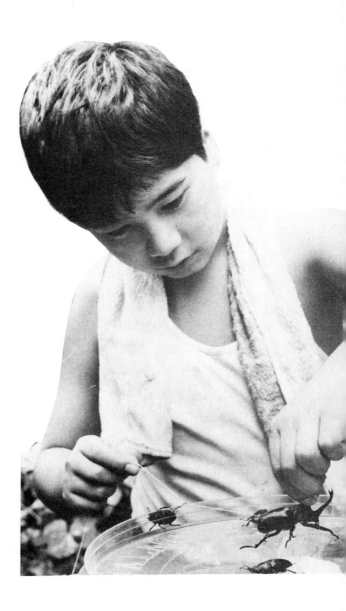

sings with a clear, metallic ring. *Matsumushi,* called the pine insect, makes sharp bursts of sound. An insect called the *katan* sings soft, trembling notes. Lucky is the boy or girl who owns a *suzumushi,* whose song sounds like the soft, clear tinkling of a bell.

Insect concerts are held on late summer evenings in parks, gardens, and on the grounds of temples. Beautiful sounds fill the air as adults and children gather with their musical pets.

The main event on these happy evenings is the ceremony of "Freeing the Insects." A hush falls over the crowd as the cages are opened. As soon as the insects realize they are free, they fly away with a burst of song.

Since the musical insects live only from spring to fall, they are freed so they can breed and lay eggs before they die. The following spring, Japanese boys and girls are rewarded with a new crop of musical insects.

## AUTHOR

Leona Meals was born in Hungary, where she learned to speak Hungarian, French, and German. When she came to live in the United States, she learned English and became especially interested in American history. She has written many articles for magazines.

# A Cane in Her Hand

by ADA B. LITCHFIELD

My name is Valerie Sindoni, and I don't use my long cane all the time.

Sometimes I don't need it. I don't need it when I go to Roger's house. He's my cousin and lives next door. I've been there so many times, I know every step of the way.

Why do I have a long cane? Because I can't see very well — that's why. But I haven't always had a cane.

I *have* always worn thick glasses to help me see. But one day I found that, even with my glasses, I wasn't seeing well.

I couldn't find my new jeans when I got up. I banged into the door and hurt my knee.

After breakfast, I went outside. I saw something moving in Roger's yard. It was Roger with his little sister Ruthie behind him. They were coming out of a gray fog. "That's strange," I thought. I knew it wasn't a foggy day.

I ran toward them. But I stubbed my toe and fell.

"Hey," Roger yelled. "Look where you're going. You blind or something?"

"I guess so," I said, pushing myself up and feeling around for my glasses.

To tell the truth, I *was* having trouble seeing. Everything kept disappearing in a fog.

Ruthie said, "Don't worry, Val. Let's play."

But I was worried. I had a sharp pain in my left eye.

Like the fog, the pain came and went.

"I'm going home," I yelled at Roger.

"Hey, Val!" Roger bellowed, chasing after me. "Come back and play! I didn't mean that about being blind."

"Forget it," I told him and ran into my house and slammed the door.

My mother was worried when I told her about the pain. She made me go to my room and lie down. "Rest your eyes," she said. "I think the pain will stop."

After she helped me to bed, I heard her go downstairs and call my father and the doctor.

I didn't go to school on Monday. Instead, I went with Mom and Dad to see Dr. King. He was glad to see me, and that made me feel better. He took me into a room where he'd tested my eyes before.

Dr. King asked me questions. Did my eyes sting? Were they watery? Did bright lights make them hurt?

I pointed to my left eye. "This one hurts," I said. "I just can't see through the fog."

Then Dr. King put drops in my eyes. He had me sit in the waiting room while he talked with my parents.

Soon the nurse led me back to Dr. King. He spent some time flashing bright lights in my eyes.

"Am I going to have to go to the hospital?" I asked. I'd had an operation on my right eye when I was little. It hadn't helped much. I still couldn't see very well with that eye.

"I don't think so, Val," the doctor said. "But I will have to check your eyes every few days." I thought he sounded worried. That made me worried too.

"Am I going to be blind, Dr. King?" I asked. I felt like crying.

"We hope not, Val," he said slowly. "We're going to do all that we can to keep that from happening."

Soon Mom was holding my hand. She said, "Dr. King wants us to talk to your teacher, Val. She can help you at school."

"She already does," I said. "She lets me go right up to the chalkboard to see stuff. She gives me books with large print to read. And special paper with black lines and a special pencil too. What else can Mrs. Johnson do?"

"We'll have to find out," my father said.

When Dr. King said it was okay, I went back

to school. Mom went with me. She talked to Mrs. Johnson and other people.

It was a bad time. Lessons are hard when you can't see well. And I kept bumping into things, even when I tried my best to see what was in the way.

Then one Monday, Mrs. Johnson told me, "Miss Sousa is here. She's the special teacher for children who have trouble seeing. She helps with lessons. She'll also teach you how to travel by yourself so you won't get lost or hurt."

It sounded like it might be all right. But I hated to go to another room and leave my friends, even for a little while.

After Mrs. Johnson went back to the other kids, Miss Sousa gave me a test. She showed me some book pages. I read out loud those I could see.

Then we talked about how people who can't see well get around — by listening carefully, by touching, and by feeling with their hands and with their whole bodies sometimes. These were things I'd been doing for a long time without thinking about it.

I saw Miss Sousa two days a week after that. She helped me with schoolwork. She showed me how to hold my hands and arms so I wouldn't run smack into things I didn't see. I liked Miss Sousa. She's so nice you can't help liking her. I began to think going to her room wasn't so bad.

Then one day Miss Sousa held something out to me. It was a long cane.

"Oh, no!" I shouted. "I don't need that. Only blind people use canes. I'm not blind. I don't want it."

Miss Sousa didn't get mad. She said, "You know, Val, you're getting a lot of bumps lately. It's because you don't see some of the low things in your way. Your hands and arms don't reach far enough."

Well, that was true. It's no fun running into things. It hurts and it makes you feel stupid. I could use some help.

Miss Sousa put the cane in my hand. "A long cane is like a long arm," she said. "With it, you will find the low things before you bump into them."

"A long, skinny arm," I said, and Miss Sousa laughed.

She went on, "I've moved things around in here. I'm going to the other side of the room. I want you to follow me. Use your eyes and ears. Walk slowly. Use the cane as if it were your hand to find anything in your way."

I tried a few steps and moved the cane from side to side in front of me.

*Ping!* The cane hit the trash basket. I knew it was the trash basket by the sound it made. So I used the cane to find enough space to walk around it.

*Plunk!* A heavy chair. *Plink!* The leg of a metal table. I walked around everything.

"How about that!" Miss Sousa said. "You followed me across the room and didn't bump into anything." I felt sort of proud. But I didn't like the noise the cane made and the way it felt in my hand. Still, it was fun to guess what things were from the sounds they made.

"Do you know what you were doing?" Miss Sousa asked. "You were cane traveling. It's not easy. Let me show you how to use your cane so it won't be so noisy and clumsy."

In the next weeks Miss Sousa taught me how to hold and use a long cane to travel indoors. I was glad we practiced in her room. It was easier with just the two of us. Each time, she put more things in my way. I learned to tell what was in my way by the sound it made and by how it felt when I touched it with the cane. Then I found how to go around it.

"Val," Miss Sousa said one day, "you're getting to be a very good cane traveler." She made it sound like being a good swimmer or skater. Then she said, "Let me know when you want to practice in the hall."

I wasn't sure I liked that idea. In the room it was okay, but maybe people in the hall wouldn't understand. How about my friends?

Well, they understood! It didn't make any difference to them. Miss Sousa had me practice going from my room to the gym and to the music room. I had my own cane now.

Later, I took my cane outdoors and learned how to find the edge of the walk or a hedge or a fence to help me stay on the path. Miss Sousa stayed right with me.

Now my long cane takes lots of bumps for me. I use it at school, especially going to different rooms. I take it with me when I go places. I don't often go to new places alone. But someday I will, and my cane will keep me from bumping into things or falling when I come to a curb.

Do I mind not being able to see as well as other kids? Yes, I do. But what I mind most is having people talk about me as if I'm not there.

One day I went to the store for Mom. Mrs. Wong, who owns the store, was talking to a woman whose voice I didn't know.

The woman saw my cane and said, "She's such a pretty girl. Too bad she can't see."

That hurt! It made me mad too. Didn't she think I could hear her? Or did she think I was too stupid to understand?

Mrs. Wong understood. It made her mad too. She knows there are lots of things a kid can do without being able to see very well. She knows I can do most things kids in my neighborhood do.

I roller-skate. (Maybe I fall down sometimes, but so does everybody.) I swim. (At camp I won a medal for swimming.) I paint pictures and make things out of clay. I am learning to play the organ. I take dancing lessons.

I have learned to do many things. And like other kids, I'm going to learn a lot more. Miss Sousa says the most important thing I'm learning is to think for myself.

I wish other people would learn that too. Then they'd know there are lots of ways of seeing. Seeing with your eyes is important, but it isn't everything.

## AUTHOR

Ada Litchfield started writing for fun when she was twelve, and she has been writing and working with books ever since. She has been an editor for book publishers and a teacher. She and her husband, both fond of cats and gardening, live in Massachusetts.

While writing scripts for a TV series, Mrs. Litchfield found that there were few books for young readers about children with seeing problems, so she decided to write *A Cane in Her Hand.* Another of her books, *A Button in Her Ear,* tells about a girl who cannot hear well.

# A Picture Map

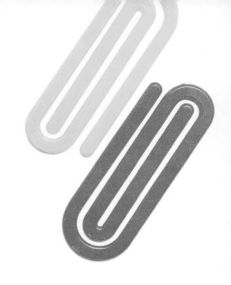

A map is a kind of picture that tells about the surface of the earth. A map can show all the earth's surface or just a small part, such as a town or a park. A map can help you to learn more about the town you live in. It can also help you to learn about places you have never seen.

Maps can be very useful in planning trips. By using a map, you can decide which route to take to get to a certain place. You can see which route is the shortest or which route passes through another place you may want to visit.

Look at the map on the next page. This map is called a **picture map.** The title at the top of the map tells you that it is a map of a town called Riverton. This picture map shows you several things about Riverton. It shows street names, such as Main Street. It shows buildings, such as the

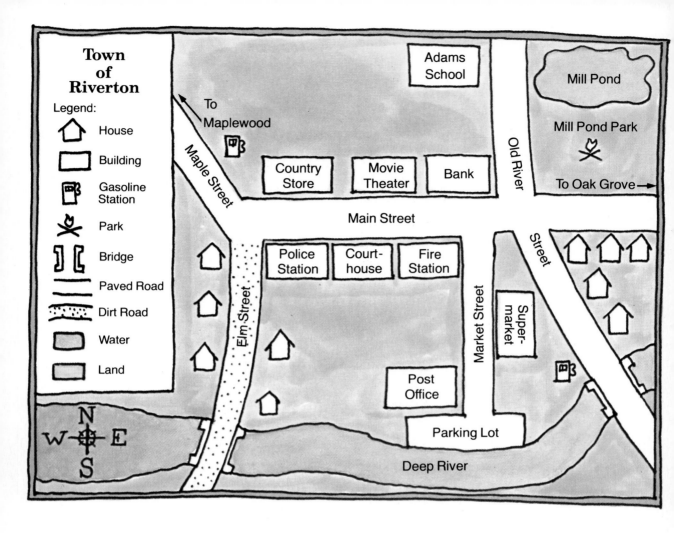

courthouse and the country store. It also shows certain places, such as the bridge on Old River Street. Try to find these four places on the map.

Most maps have what is called a **legend,** or map key. The legend tells you what each symbol on the map represents, or stands for. Most legends are in a box in a corner of the map. The legend for the map of Riverton is, as you can see, in the upper left-hand corner of the map.

Look at the symbols listed in this legend, and then look at the map. You will see that you can understand all the symbols used in this picture map by checking the legend. Notice that color is also used as a symbol on this map. Blue stands for water, and brown stands for land.

Another symbol found on most maps is shaped like a cross and is called a **compass rose.** On this map, the compass rose is below the legend. The letters *N, S, E,* and *W* stand for the directions north, south, east, and west. The compass rose tells which areas shown on the map are to the north, which are to the south, to the east, and to the west. You may have heard people give directions by saying something such as "Go north on Route 9 and then east on Highway 1." If you did not know which way was north or east, you could end up traveling in the wrong direction! Look at the map of Riverton again, and see if the Adams School is north, south, east, or west of Main Street.

If you were a stranger visiting Riverton, you would find it useful to have a picture map of the town. Then you would have no trouble finding places and would not have to worry about getting lost.

## REVIEW

1. What is a map?

2. Why are maps useful when you are planning a trip?

3. What does the legend on a map tell you about the map?

4. What does the compass rose on a map tell you about the map?

5. On which street in Riverton are the courthouse and the country store?

6. What river does the bridge on Old River Street cross?

7. In which direction is the Adams School from Main Street?

# READING A PICTURE MAP

Use the picture map of Riverton on page 214 to answer each of the following questions:

1. On which street is the post office?
2. Which street in Riverton is a dirt road?
3. On which two streets in Riverton are there gasoline stations?
4. What is the name of the land that is around Mill Pond?
5. If you lived on Elm Street, which streets would you travel on to get to the Adams School?
6. If you wanted to walk from the parking lot at the end of Market Street to the bank, in which direction would you walk?

# The Lion

There was a lion . . .
What kind of lion?
Very ferocious,
Grim and atrocious.
How terrible, how terrible!

Don't ask what he ate —
If he liked it . . . too late!
A tram and a track,
A cloud for a snack.
How terrible, how terrible!

He stepped with three legs,
He watched with three eyes,
He listened with three ears.
How terrible, how terrible!

Sharp teeth, evil eye,
He'd pass nothing by.
How terrible, how terrible!

Brana one day
Rubbed him away
With his eraser.
How terrible, how terrible!

by DUSAN RADOVIC

# Dance of the Animals

a Puerto Rican folktale by PURA BELPRÉ

Once upon a time, a Lion and a Lioness lived together near a great forest and had for neighbors such couples as Señor (seh–nyor′) Horse and Señora (seh–nyor′ah) Mare, Señor and Señora Donkey, Señor Bull and Señora Cow, Señor and Señora Dog, and Señor and Señora Goat.

Times were bad for them, and soon the day came when they faced each other with nothing in the house to mix for a meal.

"We must do something," said the Lioness. "If times keep up like this, we shall certainly perish, a thing which should not happen, for are we not the strongest beasts in the forest? Has it not been said that the biggest fish shall eat the smaller?"

"True enough," answered the Lion. "Something must be done." And he set to thinking for a while.

"I have it," said he, after a while, "and a splendid idea it is, even if I have to say it myself! Listen. Which meat do we like the best?"

"Goat's meat," answered Señora Lioness.

"Right," said the Lion. "It is the finest, the juiciest, and certainly the tastiest.

"Ah, *Señora mía* (seh–nyor′ah mee′ah), you shall see," explained the Lion.

"But how are we going to get such fresh and delicious meat?" asked the Lioness. "To hear you talk, one would think we are kings."

"I will tell you," said Señor Lion. "Listen carefully. We shall give a ball, a grand ball, and to it we shall invite our friends. You who are so well liked will invite our neighbors, and they will not refuse. Outside the back door we will build a fire. When the dance begins and everyone is on the floor, I will push the goat and cast him into the fire. The rest depends on me. How do you like my plan?"

Señora Lioness thought for a while, shaking

her head slowly at first as if the plan did not meet with her approval. Then, suddenly realizing what it all meant, she exclaimed, "Oh, most generous idea! Meat at last."

"You will have to hurry if my plans are to be carried out," said Señor Lion.

Señora Lioness went out to invite the neighbors, while Señor Lion stayed home to prepare the house for the big affair.

"*Hola* (oh'lah)! Señora Mare," exclaimed Señora Lioness, as she came upon her in the forest.

"*Hola!* Señora Lioness! What are you doing around these parts, my good friend?"

"I came to invite you to a dance at our house. You and Señor Horse have such fine long legs and such strong hoofs. We need you for our orchestra. Could you not come and play the drum?"

"Oh, most certainly," answered Señora Mare. "Only yesterday was I saying that we needed a little recreation. Yes, we will come and play the drum!"

"*Gracias* (grah′see–ahs)," said Señora Lioness and went her way.

Pretty soon she found Señora Donkey.

"Ah, *amiga mía* (ah–mee′gah mee′ah)," said she, greeting her friend. "I was just going to your house. We are giving a ball and would like to have you and Señor Donkey come. Señor Horse and Señora Mare are coming to play the drum. Won't you and Señor Donkey come and play the trombone?"

"Why, yes, Señora Lioness, we will be there without fail."

"*Gracias! Gracias!*" said Señora Lioness. "You see, your voices are so rich that without their resonance our ball would be a failure. . . ."

On went Señora Lioness, faster and faster as she felt the pangs of hunger in her empty stomach. She had not had goat's meat in such a long time. She crossed lane after lane, inviting here and there, and giving each invitation with such graciousness that those invited felt that the dance would not be a success unless they accepted.

When she reached Señor and Señora Dog's house, she found them sitting under the shade of a great tree.

"*Hola amigos!*" cried she, a little breathless, for she had walked quite a distance now and her throat was beginning to feel dry after so much talking.

"There is a great ball at my house tonight. You both must come," said Señora Lioness.

"I will go," said the dog, "but Señora Dog stays home."

"I will go, too," said Señora Dog quickly.

"No, no," shrieked Señor Dog.

"*Sí* (see), *sí,*" yelled Señora Dog.

"Oh, my friends," said Señora Lioness, hurriedly, "I must leave you to decide the matter yourselves. I must call at Señor Goat's house."

"Wait, Señora Lioness! Señor Goat is my best friend. I will take you there," said Señor Dog.

Once at Señor Goat's house, Señor Dog drew him aside and suggested that he should go alone to the dance.

It was done as he said. So Señora Dog and Señora Goat missed Señora Lioness's ball.

Señora Lioness left with a sad heart, for Señor Goat would not render enough meat for two.

Why did she have to invite the dog first? Why didn't she ignore him just this once? What would Señor Lion say when he heard that only Señor Goat was coming? Señor Goat, so thin and lanky!

She soon reached home. Señor Lion had straightened things, and outside the door a large bonfire flared. On a tripod hung a large earthenware pot. Señora Lioness heard the water sizzle and reach the boiling point. She hurried in.

"Well, you are here at last," cried the Lion. "Are they all coming?"

"Yes, all — that is, except —— "

She never finished the sentence, for so excited was Señor Lion that he danced around the house for joy and then went out to tend the fire.

Señora Lioness had hardly finished placing a garland of coffee flowers on her neck when the first guests arrived.

"*Buenos días* (bway'nohs dee'ahs)," said she, greeting Señor and Señora Donkey. The new-comers looked spotlessly clean, and in order to play freely, they had refrained from wearing ornaments.

"What a beautiful garland!" exclaimed Señor Donkey. "And how becoming!"

"*Gracias,* my friend," answered Señora Lioness.

Another pair came along. This time it was Señor and Señora Cat.

"Oh!" exclaimed Señora Lioness, a note of admiration in her voice. "What an adorable necklace!"

Señora Cat had woven honeysuckle and pinned a bunch around her neck on a blue rib-bon. She looked like a flower herself, her beautiful eyes dancing for pure joy. Her white fur stood out as if it had been freshly brushed. As she moved about, the delicate scent of honey-suckle spread, perfuming the air.

When Señor Bull and Señora Cow appeared, they were as pretty as a picture. From the river

they came, yet dry and shining! They had threaded gray and red chaplets around their horns. The tan of their hides had a lustrous shine and the gray and red of the berries stood out against the black of their large, soft eyes.

Last came Señor Dog and Señor Goat.

"And the Señoras?" inquired Señor Lion. "Aren't they coming?"

"No," said Señor Goat.

"Oh, no!" said Señor Dog.

"My dear," whispered Señor Lion to Señora Lioness, "we shall have to eat them both, since Señora Goat did not come."

Like Señor and Señora Donkey, Señor Goat and Señor Dog wore no ornaments; but their guilt in leaving their respective wives at home showed in their faces.

Motioning to the orchestra to begin, Señor Lion and Señora Lioness opened the dance. The couples whirled, stamped, and bellowed. What tangoes and *jotas* (hoh′tahs)! Waltzes mingled with mazurkas and traditional dances. And the orchestra! Never had there been one like it! Señora Ant played the guitar. The drum was placed in such a convenient place that Señor

Horse had no difficulty in striking it with his hoofs as he danced around.

What a resonance! Señor Dog barked and howled. Señor and Señora Cat miaowed, while the constant stamping of Señor Donkey and the bombarding brays of Señora Mare filled the place. On and on the couples danced until the floor creaked under the weight of their bodies.

Suddenly on one of the turns of a dance, Señor Goat and Señor Dog, who for lack of partners were dancing together, spied the bonfire outside the door.

"*Amigo,*" said the goat, "I do not like the look of that fire. Let us go, for this bonfire is meant for us and so is the pot of boiling water hanging over it. No doubt, Señor Lion means to eat us up."

Through the dancing couples they pulled and pushed, skipping all the time until they reached the farther door. Once out, they ran as fast as their legs could carry them, looking back now and then to see if they were being followed.

Meanwhile, at the ball, things went on as before. Suddenly Señor Lion missed Señor Dog and Señor Goat. As quickly as he could, without causing suspicion, he left the house.

The afternoon was cool and the air was heavy with the scent of the acacia trees in full bloom. The wind began to blow and with it a sprinkle of rain, which came slowly at first and then in great torrents. On and on ran Señor Lion, and coming out at the turn of the road, he spied Señor Dog and Señor Goat, running ahead of him. Faster and faster ran the Lion, yet faster went Señor Dog and Señor Goat.

They soon reached the river. It was swollen with the sudden downpour. The dog was not afraid and swam across, but the goat did not know what to do. Looking back he saw Señor Lion coming closer and closer.

"Oh, for a good place of safety!" he said.

As he turned around, he spied a large bunch of hay. He quickly got under it and rolled himself until only his tail stuck out. Presently Señor Lion reached the shore.

"Where have they gone?" exclaimed he. He heard a sharp call. He looked across the river, and there he saw Señor Dog happily jumping and mocking him. Señor Lion snarled and showed his fangs. If he could only swim across, he thought, he could show this impudent dog what he could do. But he could not, and what was more humiliating, Señor Dog knew it too.

"You are so clever and quick," called the dog across the river. "Why don't you swim? Surely the current will help you."

Señor Lion was furious. Swim indeed!

"I'll make your babbling tongue stop," he called back.

He looked around. The place was full of stones. He picked up one and hurled it at the dog

across the river. Señor Dog saw it coming and jumped out of reach.

"Oh, my friend," he called, "see the bundle of straw near you? Why don't you try and throw a stalk of that at me?"

"One stalk, indeed," roared Señor Lion, fully realizing that Señor Dog was making fun of his strength. "I will throw you the pack."

So saying, he leaned forward and tried to pull at the pack, which, besides being slippery because of the rain, was quite heavy with the weight of the goat inside of it. No sooner had he pulled at it than he slipped and fell on his back.

At this, Señor Dog leaped up and barked for joy. "Try again, my friend," he called at Señor Lion.

Señor Lion stood up and went at the straw pack again. He pulled and pulled, and finally raising it, he hurled it across the river. No sooner did it land on the ground than Señor Goat jumped out of his hiding place and, accompanied by Señor Dog, began to cut capers in the air.

"Señor Lion," he called, "thanks for ferrying me over. If I did lose my tail, my life indeed I saved!"

Señor Lion's rage had no limit, and looking down at his paws, he discovered that he had a large amount of fur entangled in his claws. Then he laughed and answered:

"So you have, my friend, but by your stump you'll tell your tale."

And it is true, because even to this day, goats have only a stump for a tail.

# AUTHOR

"Storytelling was a natural pastime as I grew up in Puerto Rico," says Pura Belpré. The folktales she heard as a child were to become important to her later in life.

As a young woman, she came from Puerto Rico to visit New York and stayed there to go to library school. Later she became a children's librarian.

When Pura Belpré tells stories to children, she uses puppets to make the stories even more enjoyable. Since childhood she has been interested in puppets. Back then she used to make her own out of fruit or whatever else was around.

Pura Belpré's storytelling has entertained New York children and has been valuable for them as well. By telling Spanish-speaking newcomers familiar old stories in Spanish, she has made them feel at home in their new land.

Other books you might enjoy by this author are *The Rainbow-Colored Horse, Juan Bobo and the Queen's Necklace,* and *Oté: A Puerto Rican Folk Tale.* In all her work, she shares with all children the rich culture of Puerto Rico.

# How About That!

*About* — it's a simple word. You probably use it fifty times a day. Did you ever think of all the ways in which you can use it?

Do you remember Granny in "Brave Janet of Reachfar"? Tom and George, who worked on the farm, said that Granny had her *"on abouts."* What did they mean? They meant that Granny had times when she told everybody just what she thought. You may never have used *about* in quite that way before. But *about* is used in this story in other ways too.

Look at page 166. The last sentence in the second paragraph ends with ". . . Tom and George, who did most of the work *about* the farm." Now look at page 178. Tom says, "We are going to be late for tea. Herself will be so angry *about* that. . . ." Does *about* have the same meaning in both sentences?

What does *about* mean in the sentence on page 166? Yes, it means "around."

Does *about* have the same meaning in the sentence on page 178? No, Herself would not be angry *around* something. *About* here means "having to do with," as in the following sentence:

**We are reading stories** *about* **animals.**

This is the meaning of *about* that you've probably heard and read most often.

There is another way in which we use *about*. What does it mean in this sentence?

**I have** *about* **fifty cents left.**

It means "more or less" or "roughly." It is the opposite of *exactly*.

There are many more meanings for *about*. You might want to look them up in a dictionary. Then you will know just about all there is to know about *about!*

# Books to Enjoy

**The Desert Is Theirs** by Byrd Baylor
The world of the Papago Indians is the desert and all the living things in it.

**Bright Lights to See By**
by Miriam Anne Bourne
How exciting it was when electricity was first used to light Maggie's father's hotel!

**Sports Hero: Muhammad Ali**
by Marshall Burchard
This biography of a boxing champion has interesting photographs and is easy to read.

**Engine Number Seven** by Eleanor Clymer
When their Maine town is snowbound, Dot and Sam save an old train from being destroyed.

**Save That Raccoon!** by Gloria D. Miklowitz
A raccoon escapes from a dangerous forest fire.

**Anna's Silent World** by Bernard Wolf
Anna is a young deaf girl who leads a fun-filled, active life.

# Weavers

MAGAZINE THREE

# Contents

# Josephine's 'Magination

by ARNOLD DOBRIN

"If you're going with me to market, you better get a move on," Josephine's mother called.

Josephine put down her flower dolls and brushed the dirt off her skirt. She rushed into the house to get a drink of water, tried to brush some more dirt off her dress, and then ran down the path. Already her mother was turning the bend in the road past the palmettos. Her back was straight as a board because on her head she carried the big basket of brooms she took to market each Friday morning.

Oh, it was hot — it was terribly hot! And it would be that way for a long time. It would stay that way through most of the day. But then, when the shadows started to get big, a cool, soft breeze would gently drift in from the sea. And that would feel so good.

About that time — if all the brooms were sold — Josephine's mother would give her some pennies to spend on whatever she wanted. Candy? Sweet jellied-rolls? It was always hard for Josephine to decide. But it was awfully nice to think about on and off throughout the day.

"*Bonjour* (bohn-zhoor′), Lucille," said a woman who suddenly came out of a path on her way to town. She carried a heavy load of fruit to sell, and already she looked hot.

"*Bonjour*, Francoise (frahn-swahz′)," called Josephine's mother.

"Going to be a very hot day," Francoise sighed.

"It's going to be that, all right," Josephine's mother said as they walked, single file, down the dusty path. As they talked, Josephine fell behind. She let her feet move slowly in the warm, soft dust of the path and thought about those pennies she might get at the end of the day.

It would be nice to buy a doll — a real doll. Josephine had never had a real doll. She'd had flower dolls — like the ones she'd played with that morning. But they were just hibiscus-flower dolls.

Her mother had showed her how to make them when she was very small. She showed her how to take a tiny sliver of wood and stick it into a hibiscus bud. That was the head. The rest of the stick went into a big flower turned upside down. That made the skirt.

They were pretty, yes, and delicate too. But they wilted so soon. Josephine would make them fresh and bright in the morning, but by noon their heads would shrivel and their skirts would look torn and shaggy.

Josephine wished she could have a real doll someday.

After a while, another woman turned into the dusty path with a load of baskets. *"Bonjour, Lucille,"* she called to Josephine's mother.

*"Bonjour,* Gabrielle (gah–bree–ell´),*"* came the answer.

In a little while they met a man with a wheelbarrow full of grain. Soon they met other men too — men with burros or goats. One man tugged at a stubborn pig. Everybody had something to sell at the market. Nobody went with empty hands — except Josephine. When you go to market, you've got to have something to sell.

Around the bend in the road, Josephine could smell the market place. It was a good smell of fruit and vegetables, of candies and frying pork, of goats and pigs, and of straw and dust.

Josephine walked faster now. She followed her mother to their favorite spot in a little patch of shade under a torn awning. Carefully Josephine's mother lowered the basket of little brooms from her head and set it before her as she sat down. Now her shop was in order. She didn't have one thing more to do except sit and sell brooms until the sun went down.

"Now you run off, child," Josephine's mother said as she gave her a playful little push. "I have business to attend to."

Josephine wandered through the big, noisy market. All along the sides of the square were little shops where people were busy buying or selling or cooking or making things.

Josephine had just turned away from the butcher shop when she bumped into an old man she had never seen before. He had a big stick and a very big straw hat — much bigger than anyone else's hat. On his hat were

different animals made of straw. There were monkeys and pigs, donkeys and roosters. Some of them had tiny, jingly bells attached or were decorated with bright strips of cloth.

"Looks like you have bumped into good luck, young lady!" The old man cackled and pulled one of the little straw pigs off his hat. "Here, child," he said, "I don't want to see those big, frightened eyes of yours first thing

this market day. I want to start off with a *smile*.
Come on now, child. Let me see a good big
smile. That's the *only* way to start off market
day!"

Josephine smiled and said, "Thank you," as
she took the pretty thing in her hand. She was
about to run to her mother when she had a
thought. She turned to the old man, saying,
"How did you learn to make little animals of
straw like that?"

"Why, child," he said good-naturedly, "nobody taught me how to do it. Nobody taught me how to do much of anything. I just used my 'magination!"

Toward afternoon the shadows started to get big. The cool, soft breeze started to drift in from the sea. Josephine ran back to where her mother was sitting in the shade of the torn awning.

"Look, *Maman* (mah–mahn'), look what a man gave me!"

Josephine's mother took the pig and examined it closely. "Cute little thing," she said, but then she sighed wearily. Josephine saw that only about half of the brooms were gone. "Guess we better start getting home," her mother said as she felt around for her hat. "This just isn't much of a broom day!" But then she reached for the little black bag where she kept her money. She pulled out a penny — just one penny. "I guess you need something sweet in your mouth before we start for home. Now — run off to that Fine Sweet Shop."

Josephine rushed to the candy and cake store. On her way she passed the stall where

the dolls were sold. But she tried not to look at them, tried not to think about them. For one penny she could get only one piece of candy so she chose carefully. Finally she decided on a nice piece of hard, lime candy — tangy but sweet, and cool like the breeze that was softly blowing in from the sea.

The sun was setting. The wind from the sea grew stronger. Josephine thought that this was one of the best times of market day — just going home. In the east, the moon hung in the sky like a big, pale slice of melon. The palmettos whispered and scratched against each other in the evening sea breeze.

As soon as Josephine got home, she ran to see her flower dolls. They were so wilted and ugly that she was sorry she had kept them. She swept them angrily off the table onto the floor and went to help her mother prepare dinner.

They ate baked yams, breadfruit, and mangoes, and then had sugar cane. Josephine was so hungry that every bite tasted delicious. "Never saw a child eat so much in my life!" her mother said.

But after she had eaten, the only thing that she could think about was her bed. Lying down in a darkened corner of the room, she thought about the happy old man with the straw toys attached to his big hat. How clearly she could hear him saying in a laughing voice, "I just used my 'magination!"

Did Josephine have a 'magination? Maybe she did and maybe she didn't. Just before she went to sleep she promised herself that she wouldn't let another day pass without finding out if she, too, had a 'magination.

The morning was still cool when Josephine awoke. She looked at the bright, long stripes of morning sunlight falling on the floor of their one-room house. In the far corner of the room, her mother was sleeping soundly on her bed of straw matting. Outside, the birds were busy calling out to each other and getting their breakfasts.

That made her remember. She, too, should be getting busy. She had to find out about her 'magination.

Josephine looked around the room again and again. She tried to make some 'magination thoughts come into her head. She tried very hard to think. To see if she could find something — or *two* different things — that she could make something *new* out of.

There in a corner were short, broken broom handles. Nearby were the scratchy straw parts of the brooms — and scissors and raffia. Josephine looked at them for a long time.

Then, almost before she knew what she was doing, Josephine jumped out of bed and tied one of the straw brooms to a broken broom handle. Then she took scissors and cut the straws short.

How funny it looked now — not like a broom
at all but like a skirt.

Without even thinking what she was doing,
Josephine ran to the shed where her mother
kept some rags and paint. She tore one rag
into strips. Then she wrapped the strips tightly
round and round and tucked the ends in. She
glued the smooth rag ball to the top of the
broom handle. After the glue dried, she took an
old brush and quickly covered the broom handle and the rag ball with black paint. She

253

worked quickly without thinking very much how. She knew what she had to do. Something was telling her. She knew it was her 'magination giving out orders.

As soon as the paint had dried, Josephine took some brightly colored scraps of cloth that were left over from a dress Josephine's mother had made for her. One of the strips got tied around the middle of the broom-doll. The other was bound around its head in the same

way that some women on the island bound their heads.

Josephine put the broom-doll down and looked at it. It was amazing what 'magination could tell you to do — no doubt about it! But something important was still missing. Josephine picked a long, feathery weed that made a fine-pointed brush. A dab of red made the mouth. White showed where the eyes were.

Oh, yes, now she was wonderful. She was a doll, a *real* doll. But she was more than a doll too. Just take her in your fingers and brush her back and forth and she worked hard cleaning and sweeping for you! What a good, busy kind of doll — not just one that lay around the house all day waiting to be taken care of.

"Show me what you got there!" her mother's voice suddenly commanded from the doorway.

"I made a doll, *Maman,*" Josephine said, taking the broom-doll to show her mother.

"Well . . . I never saw such a thing before." Her mother smiled. "Why, Josephine, you made yourself a mighty cute little doll."

"And *Maman,*" Josephine said, "she's a good worker too!" She showed her mother what a good sweeping her doll could do.

"Yes — and a good worker too!" her mother agreed. "Josephine — you're a mighty smart little girl."

That afternoon they decided to make more broom-dolls so they could take them to market on Friday morning. Josephine's mother made the brooms as usual, but Josephine painted their faces. And part of her job was also to tie the brightly colored pieces around their middles and on their heads.

When Friday morning came, Josephine and her mother were out of bed early and on their way into town while the morning was still cool. Hardly anyone was at the market place when they arrived. And it seemed that hours and hours went by — a long, long time — until anyone even came to see the strange little broom-dolls.

But then people began to come to look at them. And after they touched and admired the dolls, they began to buy them. The children came, too, and begged their parents to buy some dolls. To them it didn't matter that the dolls were such good workers. They just liked the way the dolls looked.

Josephine watched with delight as the little black purse began to fill with coins. She was just thinking about what she would choose as a treat when she saw a big shadow on the ground before her.

It was the shadow of the big straw hat that the old toy man wore. First he looked at the brooms, then at Josephine. He said, "I know you. You're the girl who bumped into me the other day."

"Yes, I'm the girl," Josephine said.

The toy man's smile broadened. "And you made these dolls? I've never seen such dolls before!"

"My mother and I made them," Josephine said.

He took one and turned it around admiringly. "Child — I'd say you got a powerful 'magination."

Josephine smiled.

## AUTHOR

Arnold Dobrin says that when he was in the third grade in Los Angeles, he began to think of himself as an artist. He loved the wonderful designs he could make on paper with paintbrushes. After going to art school, he worked as an art designer for movie studios. Then he became a writer.

Mr. Dobrin has traveled and lived in various parts of the world and has written about most of these places. Among his books are *Taro and the Sea Turtles, Gilly Gilhooley: a Tale of Ireland, Scat!* and *Jillions of Gerbils.*

# Your Busy Brain

by

LOUISE GREEP McNAMARA
and
ADA BASSETT LITCHFIELD

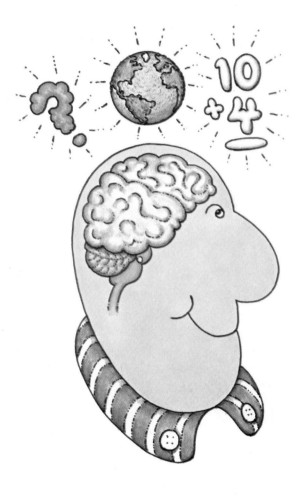

Everybody says Maria is a brain. What do they mean? They mean Maria uses her brain well.

She uses her brain, as you use yours, to learn, to daydream, to ask questions, to solve problems, to make choices, and to make sense of the world around her.

Without a brain, Maria could do none of these things. And neither could you.

Put your hands on your head. You know where your brain is, but do you know what it looks like? If you could look inside your head, you would see a soft, wrinkled, pinkish-gray thing that fills most of the space in your skull. Feel the hard

Adapted from *Your Busy Brain* by Louise Greep Mc-Namara and Ada Bassett Litchfield. Published by Little, Brown and Company.

bones. Like a built-in crash helmet, your skull bones surround your brain and protect it.

Your brain knows many things. When a fly is sitting on your nose, your brain knows it. Your brain tells the muscles in your arm to swat the fly. How does it do this?

Your brain is part of a network of nerves that runs down your spinal cord and all over your body. Your body uses this network of nerves to carry messages to and from your brain.

Message from nose to brain: A fly is sitting on me.

Message from brain to arm muscles: Swat it!

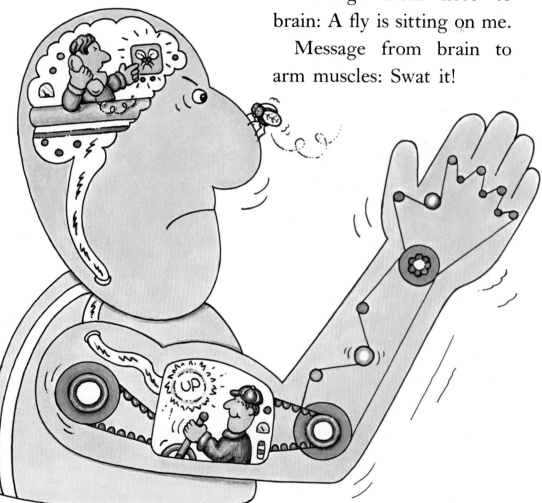

Like all the rest of you, your brain and nerves are made of cells. Some cells in your nerve network carry messages to the brain. Other nerve cells carry messages away from the brain. You might think of your brain as a giant control center, always receiving and sending messages.

Suppose you pick up a hot piece of pizza. Before the emergency message "HOT!" could go to your brain and come back to your hand, your fingers would be burned. A message from outside your body doesn't always go to your brain first. Sometimes there isn't time.

So that you won't be burned, this emergency message takes a shortcut to your spinal cord. A nerve in your spinal cord flashes back the order "DROP IT!" In an emergency like this, your hand acts first. Afterward, your brain thinks about what might have happened. When you duck a ball that comes flying at your head, the same kind of emergency shortcut takes place. Can you think of any other examples?

Your brain does more than receive and send messages. Like a big warehouse that stores many things, your brain stores a lot of information.

What do you remember? How long do you remember?

You have two kinds of memory: a short-time memory and a long-time memory. Things you do not need to remember, like a TV show you saw last night, are stored in your brain now, but may be forgotten in a few days. Things you need to remember, like your name and address and phone number, you repeat many times. Things you repeat many times usually become part of your long-time memory. Without a memory, you would have to learn the same things over and over again. You would never have time to learn new things.

Your brain is made up of three parts. The biggest part, the upper brain, is at the top of your head. This is the part of your brain with which you think and learn and solve problems.

Underneath the big part of your brain is a smaller part, the middle brain. The middle brain keeps your muscles working together smoothly. Because of it, people can walk without stumbling and talk without mumbling and draw without scribbling.

At the top of your spinal cord is the lower brain. It takes care of all the things you do without thinking, like breathing, swallowing, blinking, and digesting. It helps keep your heart beating and your blood moving.

Your brain never stops working. Even while you are sleeping, your heart is beating, your lungs are breathing, your food is digesting. And very often, the thinking part of your brain is busy dreaming. Do you remember your dreams? What do you dream about?

Nobody knows for sure why you dream. But scientists who study dreaming know that you do dream every night, whether you remember your dreams or not.

Nobody knows for sure, either, just how you learn. Some things you learn by trying, and making mistakes, and trying again. Do you remember learning to ride a bike?

Sometimes at a fair or an amusement park, you will see a house made of mirrors and glass. You are supposed to go in one door, walk through the halls, and try to find your way out. It's fun, but it isn't easy. The walls of glass and mirrors mix you up. You may have to take many wrong turns before you find the right way out.

If you could look down on a fun house, this is what you might see.

With your finger, start at the arrow and see if you can find the path you must take to get out again. Can you do it without mistakes the first time?

Try it again. It is easier the second time because some brain cells helped you remember the mistakes you made the first time you tried.

The human brain has created many wonderful things. But it is far more wonderful than anything it has ever created.

Every day you use your brain to learn what you want to learn, to do what you want to do, and to be what you want to be. It is always working for you — your own busy brain.

## AUTHORS

Louise Greep McNamara, the TV teacher for the award-winning series *All About You,* and Ada Bassett Litchfield, the script writer for *All About You,* often work together.

When the television series began, Mrs. McNamara and Mrs. Litchfield wrote some books together to explain more about how different parts of the human body work. Two of the books — *Your Busy Brain* and *Your Living Bones* — were chosen as outstanding books of science for children.

Mrs. Litchfield is also the author of *A Cane in Her Hand,* which you read earlier in this book.

# A PICTURE PUZZLE

The name NINA is hidden in this picture five times. How many NINA's can *you* find?

For many years, people have enjoyed finding the NINA's in Al Hirschfeld's picture puzzles. In this one, Mr. Hirschfeld pictured three popular old-time movie comedians, the Marx Brothers.

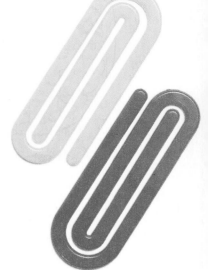

# The Topic of a Paragraph

Almost everything you read is made up of groups of sentences that are called **paragraphs.** This arrangement of sentences in paragraphs can help you when you are reading to get information.

When writing a paragraph for an informational article, a good author has in mind just one point, or thing, that the paragraph will tell about. The author makes the first sentence say something about that thing. Then each sentence that follows says something about that same thing. By the time the paragraph is finished, all the sentences in it say something about only one thing. That one thing is called the **topic** of the paragraph.

In the following paragraph, the sentences are numbered so that it will be easy for you to think about them later. As you read the paragraph, decide what thing all the sentences tell about.

1. Wherever people live, many of them have gardens.  2. Gardens may be big or small.  3. Some people have gardens mainly for beauty or fun.  4. They grow flowers like tulips and roses in their gardens.  5. Other people use gardens mainly as a way to get fresh foods.  6. They grow things like tomatoes and corn.

Sentence 1 tells where *gardens* are found.  Sentence 2 tells about the sizes of *gardens*.  Sentence 3 tells one reason people have *gardens*.  Sentence 4 tells what might be grown in those *gardens*.  Sentence 5 tells another reason people have *gardens*.  Sentence 6 tells what might be grown in those *gardens*.  You can see that each sentence says something about *gardens,* and that is why *Gardens* is the topic of the paragraph.

*Gardens* is only one word.  The topic of a paragraph may be one word or several words.  It is usually not a complete sentence. When you write the topic, you write the first word in the topic with a capital letter, like this: *Gardens.*

To find out what the topic of a paragraph is, ask yourself this question: What one thing are all the sentences in that paragraph about? Often you can do this quickly, right after you have read the paragraph. Sometimes you may have to study each sentence again to be sure.

When you do not know quickly what the topic of a paragraph is, do these things:

1. Read the first sentence again to see what it is telling about.
2. Do the same thing with each of the other sentences.
3. Then decide what one thing all the sentences are telling about. That one thing is the topic of the paragraph.

Whenever you read to get information, try to decide what the topic of each paragraph is. Doing this can help you understand and remember what each paragraph tells about.

Study the paragraph that starts below, and decide what its topic is:

In the early days of the United States, many people lived in cabins. The cabins were made from logs that were fitted together to make the walls.

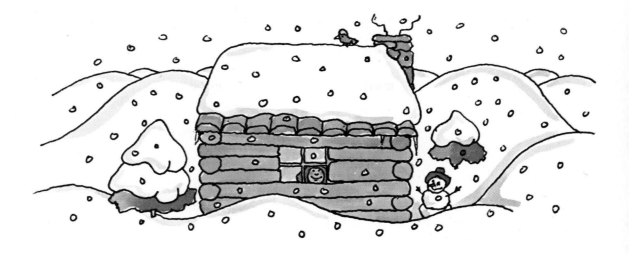

Other logs were split and used to make the roof. Usually a cabin was small and had just one or two rooms. But it was a place in which a family could stay warm and dry in the winter.

Which of the following topics is the topic of that paragraph?

1. How cabin roofs are made
2. Cabins of early settlers
3. Building cabin walls
4. The size of log cabins

**REVIEW**

1. What is meant by the *topic* of a paragraph?
2. If you cannot decide quickly what the topic of a

paragraph is, what can you do to find out what the topic is?

3. Which of the four topics listed on page 269 is the topic of the paragraph you just read? Why is each of the other topics *not* the topic of the paragraph?

## CHOOSING THE TOPIC OF A PARAGRAPH

Read the following paragraph to yourself, and decide what its topic is:

The flying squirrel does not really fly. It glides through the air. This squirrel has a fold of skin on both sides of its body that stretches from its front legs to its back legs. This skin acts like the wings of a glider and carries the animal through the air. These "wings" can carry a squirrel as much as one hundred and fifty feet, or forty-six meters.

Which of the following is the topic of that paragraph?
1. Different kinds of flying squirrels
2. How far flying squirrels glide
3. How flying squirrels move through the air
4. Why flying squirrels have wings

# The Dancers

by WALTER DEAN MYERS

"Would you like to come to work with me today, Michael?" Michael's father had put on his jacket and was picking up his tool box.

"Can I help you on your job?" Michael asked.

"No, I'm afraid not. But you can come to the theater and watch me. And if you promise to be very quiet, you can watch the dancers practice too."

So Michael went on the subway with his father to the theater.

It was Saturday morning, and the theater was empty — just rows and rows of dark, empty seats. His father led him to a seat in the first row.

"Now sit very still," he said, "and watch."

On the stage, there were people working. Some of them were moving lights around. They were the biggest lights Michael had ever seen.

Then his father and some other men began bringing trees onto the stage. The trees were made of cloth and wire, but Michael thought they looked very real. There were short trees and tall trees and even a few large rocks. It was like watching a whole forest grow in a few minutes.

After a while, some musicians came in and started playing. They didn't seem to be playing anything in particular, just making noises. Michael's father came down and sat next to him.

"What are they playing?" Michael asked.

"They aren't playing anything yet," his father said. "They're just warming up."

Then some dancers came onto the stage. They began twisting and stretching and jumping about. Then they stopped, and Michael's father whispered, "Now we have to be very quiet. They're ready to dance."

A tall man lifted his arms, and when he brought them down, all the musicians began to play. On the stage, the dancers were very still, almost like dolls. Then one of them moved, just a little. First her arm moved and her fingers spread across her face, and suddenly she was dancing.

She looked like a bird flying slowly across the stage. Michael thought that at any moment she might fly away over all their heads. Now another dancer was moving — and another — and another, until they were all dancing. They were like a flock of birds, waving their arms or gently gliding as they turned.

After a minute had passed, the music suddenly changed, and another dancer leaped onto the stage. He was bigger than the others, and Michael thought he looked like a very ferocious bird as he moved quickly about.

The ferocious bird began chasing the others, and they all flew off the stage except for the bird who had first started to fly. She tried to get away, but wherever she went, the ferocious bird followed her.

Michael could hardly sit in his chair. In front of him, the musicians were playing very fast. One of them, playing a violin, was standing as the others sat.

The ferocious bird chased the other one around and around and around until he finally caught her. Then the music changed again. It was slow now, and very sad. The lovely bird lifted her arms once more, slowly, and then fell to the ground.

The music stopped. The dancers didn't move, and for a moment it was very quiet. Then Michael stood up and clapped his hands as loudly as he could because he thought the dancing had been so good.

The dancers and the musicians all looked at Michael. The dancer who had fallen got up. She came down from the stage and came over to Michael.

"Thank you," she said, holding out her hand. "I am Yvonne. And who are you?"

"Michael."

"Do you come to the ballet often, Michael?"

"No, this is my first time. I came here with my father."

"I see. Did you like it?"

"Yes, but I'm sorry he caught you."

Yvonne smiled. "Well, just like some stories and plays, some ballets have sad endings too. You should see the entire ballet, Michael. I can get tickets for you, and I'd like you to see me dance again."

"Thank you," Michael said. "And I'd like for you to come see me at my house too. Daddy, can she come to our house?"

"I don't think so, Michael," Yvonne said. "I'm so very busy right now. I'm really sorry."

"I'm sorry too," Michael said.

"All of the dancers are very busy, Michael," his father told him. "They have to dance and practice and travel to different theaters."

"Good-by, Michael," Yvonne said, "and thank you for asking me to come to your house."

Michael said good-by to the dancers, and then he went home with his father.

One afternoon a few days later, Michael was playing Giant Steps on the sidewalk with Karen and Darlene and Jimmy. They saw a long, shiny car pulling up to the curb, right in front of Michael's house.

They stopped playing and watched as three people got out. Suddenly Michael cried, "Look! It's Yvonne!" Then Michael recognized one of the men with her. He was the dancer who had chased Yvonne on the stage, but he didn't look at all like a ferocious bird now.

"Hello, Michael," Yvonne said. "I've come to see you."

"Hello," he answered. "But how did you know where I lived?"

"The people at the theater told me where your father lived, so I knew that I would find you here too."

"I thought you would be too busy."

"I am. I told my manager I was too busy to rehearse today because I was going to see an old friend. How's that?"

"That's just fine!" Michael said, and he grinned.

"Are you really a dancer?" asked Karen, who lived next door to Michael.

"Yes, I am," Yvonne replied.

"Can you do the Chicken?" Karen asked.

"The what?"

"She doesn't dance like that, silly," Michael said. "She hops around and spins and jumps and wiggles her feet. Like this." Michael raised his hands above his head as high as he could and then spun around and jumped and tried to wiggle his feet. But he fell instead.

All the children giggled, and Karen said, "That sure must be a funny dance."

"It's really nice when *she* does it," Michael said.

"Can you do it now?" Karen asked.

"Maybe just a little." Yvonne nodded to one of the men who went to the car and brought back a violin. She and the other dancer both changed their shoes while the man with the violin got ready to play.

Then he began to play very softly, and the dancers began to dance.

"Oh, *ballet!* I *love* ballet dancing," Karen exclaimed.

They spun around and around — across the potsie squares, around the fire hydrant, and over the chalk drawings that Darlene had made on the sidewalk.

The barber came out of his shop and watched. The television repairer came out. The old man who was the super in Michael's building

sat on the top step of the stoop so he
could see better.

"Dance, Michael!" Yvonne called
out as she spun around. "Dance!"

Michael put one foot out, just a little — just a
little — and then brought it back.

"Dance, everybody, dance!" Yvonne called.

Karen put her arms out and spun slowly to the
music, and then Darlene did and Jimmy and
finally Michael. Everyone was dancing.

Up and down the stoop and around the fire hydrant and over the potsie squares they danced — and danced — and danced.

When the violin finally stopped and the dance was over, all the children clapped for the dancers and for themselves. Then Michael's mother came out and invited Yvonne and her friends upstairs for dinner. Karen came too.

Michael's house was full of collard green smells and cornbread smells and fried chicken smells. His mother and his father were smiling when they came in. The table was set with the best plates, the ones with the blue birds on them.

It was a good dinner, and everyone enjoyed it, Michael and Karen and the dancers and the violin player.

After dinner Yvonne asked Karen if she would teach her the dance that she knew. So they put on a record, and Michael and Karen did the Chicken.

Yvonne watched how Karen did it. Then she did the Chicken with Michael. Yvonne couldn't do the Chicken as well as Karen, though.

Then the violin player laughed, and the other dancer laughed.

But Yvonne hugged Karen and Michael and thanked them both for teaching her a new dance. Then she said that she had had a wonderful time but that it was time to go. Everybody said good-by, and Yvonne invited them all to the ballet.

Finally the night came when they went to the ballet. This time all the seats were filled with people, and the lights on the stage were very bright. Michael saw the violin player sitting with the other musicians.

Michael and Karen tried to sit still, but every once in a while, their arms would move with the music and their feet would wiggle under the seats. And they could almost feel that they were dancing too.

## AUTHOR

Walter Dean Myers, born in West Virginia, has written books for young people as well as stories and poems for magazines. In 1968 he was one of the first winners of the Council on Interracial Books for Children Award. *The Dancers,* which you have just read, was honored by the National Conference of Christians and Jews in 1972. Some of Mr. Myers's other books are *The Dragon Takes a Wife* and *Fly, Jimmy, Fly.*

# Unusual Friendships

by JOSE ARUEGO

Symbiosis means that two completely different kinds of animals become close friends so that they can help each other. Often they depend upon one another for survival. Here are two of these unusual friendships.

The African honey-guide loves beeswax. She can find a hive on her own but cannot break it open. So this little bird looks for the badger-like ratel and chirps to get his attention. Then she

leads him to the hive. The ratel grunts to let the bird know he is following.

Upon reaching the hive, the ratel immediately jumps on it, tears it apart with his claws, and greedily eats the honey. The angry bees try to sting the ratel, but he does not care. His thick fur and tough skin protect him.

After the ratel has finished eating the honey, he happily leaves, still surrounded by the angry bees. When they are gone, the honey-guide is finally able to get at the honeycomb and enjoy her favorite meal.

The tuatara is too lazy to build his own home. He waits around all night catching bugs while the sooty shearwater bird sleeps in the burrow she has dug for herself.

Each day, the sooty shearwater leaves her burrow to hunt for fish. As soon as she is gone, the sleepy tuatara crawls into the nest. To thank the bird for her hospitality, the tuatara rids their home of centipedes, beetles, and flies.

## AUTHOR

As a child in the Philippines, Jose Aruego was interested in humorous illustration. After becoming a lawyer, he decided to return to his childhood interest and moved to New York to study art.

Most characters in his books are animals, and he says, "It seems no matter how I draw them, they look funny." He has drawn cartoons for magazines and illustrated many children's books. Some of the books that he has both written and illustrated are *A Crocodile's Tales, Pilyo the Piranha,* and *Look What I Can Do!*

# The
# Magic
# Pumpkin

A folktale from India
by GLORIA SKURZYNSKI

Old Mother Parvati (par–vah′tee) was a Bhilla (bee′lah). The Bhillas are a brown-skinned, dark-eyed people who live on the edge of the jungle in central India. Old Mother Parvati lived all alone in a mud-walled, thatch-roofed hut in the shadow of the dark, animal-filled jungle. But she was not afraid because she had lived a long time and was very wise and because she had the gift of magic. Mother Parvati had both a magic wand and a magic pumpkin.

The magic wand looked just like any other magic wand. But the magic pumpkin was something to behold! It had a door that really opened and windows that you could see through, and it was so large that Mother Parvati could ride comfortably inside. Whenever she wanted to go somewhere, she would open the door of the magic pumpkin, step inside, and say, *"Chal ra, Bhopalla, tunuk, tunuk!"* (chal–rah′, boh–pah′la, too–nook′, too–nook′). This means, "Come on, Pumpkin, turn faster, turn faster!" And then the magic pumpkin would begin to roll along the ground, faster and faster. When it stopped, Mother Parvati would find herself wherever she wanted to be.

One day Mother Parvati decided to visit her married daughter in the village of Ghar-Bengal (gar ben–gahl′). Ghar-Bengal was quite a long distance away from Mother Parvati's hut, unless you traveled straight through the jungle, which was very, very dangerous. But Mother Parvati had a lot of confidence in her own wits and in her magic, so she decided to travel through the jungle anyway.

She arranged her hair in three long braids and wrapped a clean sari around her wiry brown body. She bundled a little pot of ghee into some jungle leaves as a gift for her daughter. Then she walked carefully through the cucumbers and eggplants and onions in her garden until she came to the enormous orange pumpkin. She opened the door and stepped inside.

*"Chal ra, Bhopalla, tunuk, tunuk!"* Mother Parvati said. The pumpkin shook until the ground rumbled. Then the big orange pumpkin began to roll, at first slowly and then faster and faster, until the pumpkin and Mother Parvati inside were rolling merrily along through the dark, mysterious jungle.

The rolling pumpkin made a loud whirring noise. Swarms of monkeys fled screaming through

the treetops overhead. Worried flocks of birds
flew straight up into the clouds. Small animals
tried to hide themselves under the jungle leaves.
But there was one great beast who wasn't frightened by the noise, and that was Vagha (vah'ga),
the great golden tiger. Curious, he padded toward
the sound. When he saw the strange whirling

pumpkin, he stopped it easily by placing his heavy golden paw on the pumpkin's lid.

Mother Parvati saw a gleaming golden eye peering at her through one of the pumpkin's windows. Then she knew that Vagha, the Emperor of the jungle, had interrupted her journey.

Calmly, the wise old lady waited for the tiger to speak because she knew exactly what she was going to do.

"Aha!" the tiger roared. "All day long I've been puzzling over what I shall eat for dinner. And now my dinner sits before me — a nice, firm, brown, juicy old lady."

In a weak, quavery voice Mother Parvati replied, "Your eyes must be failing you, O Emperor of the jungle! I am a poor, scrawny, fleshless old woman who would hardly fill a hole in your tooth." And with that, Mother Parvati waved her magic wand just a little bit, and she did become fleshless and scrawny.

"Hmmmmm," said the tiger (but when the tiger said "hmmmmm" it sounded like a roar). "Now that I look a little closer, I see that you are not as juicy a meal as I first thought. But even so, I intend to eat you for my dinner."

"But, sir, why not wait a while?" Mother Parvati said. "I'm on my way to Ghar-Bengal to visit my married daughter, who is a marvelous cook. After a week or two at her house, I'll be round and plump, a fitting meal for the Emperor of the jungle. Then, on my way back, you can eat me."

"Hmmmmm," said the tiger. "There's truth in what you say. But how do I know that you'll come back this way?"

"By the hair of Siva (see′va), I promise that I will return this way, in a week or two or three," she answered.

When the tiger heard Mother Parvati say that, he knew that he could trust her. As he lifted his heavy velvet paw from the top of the pumpkin, Mother Parvati whispered, *"Chal ra, Bhopalla, tunuk, tunuk!"* once again. The journey through the jungle continued.

Once more the noisy whirring of the magic pumpkin disturbed the jungle. Crows cawed in astonishment. The flat eyes of a cobra stared in disbelief. A leopard cub tripped over its own feet hurrying to get out of the way. But again there was one great beast who was not frightened, but only curious. Kolha (kohl′a), the gray wolf, placed his large shaggy body in the path of the pumpkin and stopped it with a thud as it hit his side.

Mother Parvati was shaken a little by the sudden stop, but she had time to recognize the rough gray coat of the great wolf.

"Aha!" said the wolf (but his "aha" sounded like "ahoooowl"). "All this long day I have

wondered what to have for supper, and now my
supper has arrived in an orange pumpkin. What
good fortune!"

"But, sir," Mother Parvati said in her weak,
quavery voice. "My poor scrawny old body could
hardly satisfy the hunger of a huge, fierce beast
like yourself." And once again she used her magic

wand to make herself look fleshless and scrawny. "I am going to Ghar-Bengal to visit my daughter, who cooks well enough to please a maharaja. After a few weeks with her, I'll be plump and delicious. Why not wait until I return from my daughter's house and eat me then?"

"But how can I be sure that you will return this way?" Kolha asked.

"By the beard of Vaghdeo (vog–day'oh), I promise to return!"

When he heard such a strong statement coming from the frail old lady, Kolha released her. Soon the whirling pumpkin was on its way again. And in less time than it takes to tell, Mother Parvati had reached the hut of her daughter, Uma (oo'ma).

Mother and daughter lived in harmony for the next few weeks, and Mother Parvati *did* get plump eating Uma's good cooking. But when it was time for Mother Parvati to return to her own home, Uma grew worried.

"Mother, I am so afraid the tiger and the wolf will be waiting to eat you," Uma said. "Please don't return through the jungle!"

But Mother Parvati only laughed. "I must return through the jungle, dear Uma. I have

given my word." Seeing her daughter's troubled look, she added, "Don't worry about me, my dear. I'm sure I am smarter than any beast in the jungle."

So into her pumpkin Mother Parvati stepped. Because she knew exactly how she would outwit the tiger and the wolf, she started the pumpkin with a *"Chal ra, Bhopalla, tunuk, tunuk."* Then she closed her eyes for a little nap.

Deep within the jungle Vagha, the tiger, had been waiting for Mother Parvati to arrive. His stomach was rumbling impatiently, and his temper was very short. As he padded back and forth along the leafy path, he mumbled grumpily to himself.

"Ho there, Vagha," the gray wolf called. "Why are you pacing the jungle in such an angry mood?"

"Ho there yourself, Kolha," the tiger replied. "I'm waiting for an old lady in a pumpkin to come along."

"How very strange!" the wolf declared. "I'm waiting for an old lady in a pumpkin myself."

"This lady is going to be my dinner," said Vagha.

"How very strange indeed!" said Kolha. "This lady is going to be my supper."

"I don't sssssuppose it could be the sssssame old lady," the tiger hissed, showing his long white teeth.

"I grrrreatly doubt it," the wolf growled, showing his sharp, pointed teeth.

"Then, sirrrr, I shall eat the firrrrst old lady who appearrrrrs," purred the sly Vagha.

"You impudent spoil-sport!" sputtered Kolha. "You mustn't spoil the splendid supper I'm expecting!"

Just then the magic pumpkin rolled into view. Kolha and Vagha both pounced on it, bringing the pumpkin to a quick halt.

With an angry wolf staring through one window and an angry tiger staring through the other, most people would have been terribly frightened. But Mother Parvati rubbed her eyes as though she had just awakened, and in a puzzled voice, she asked, "Your Excellencies, what can I do for you?"

"You promised to be my dinner," Vagha snarled.

"You promised to be *my* supper," Kolha barked. "Now which one of us is going to eat you?"

Mother Parvati shook her head and blinked her eyes. She pretended to be very confused. "Oh dear! Oh dear me," she chirped. "I do remember promising one of you that you could eat me. But which one was it? When one gets to be my age, one's memory fails, you know."

"YOU PROMISED ME!" the tiger roared.

"I WAS THE ONE SHE PROMISED!" the gray wolf howled.

The huge beasts glared at one another, their noses only an inch apart. Kolha's fierce eyes blazed like the sun, and Vagha's fierce eyes glittered like glowing coals. The rough hair along Vagha's spine rose straight up as Kolha slowly sank on his haunches, preparing to leap. And then they sprang at one another. The stillness of the jungle was filled with thuds, thumps, hisses, howls, screeches, shrieks, rattles, and roars as the animals

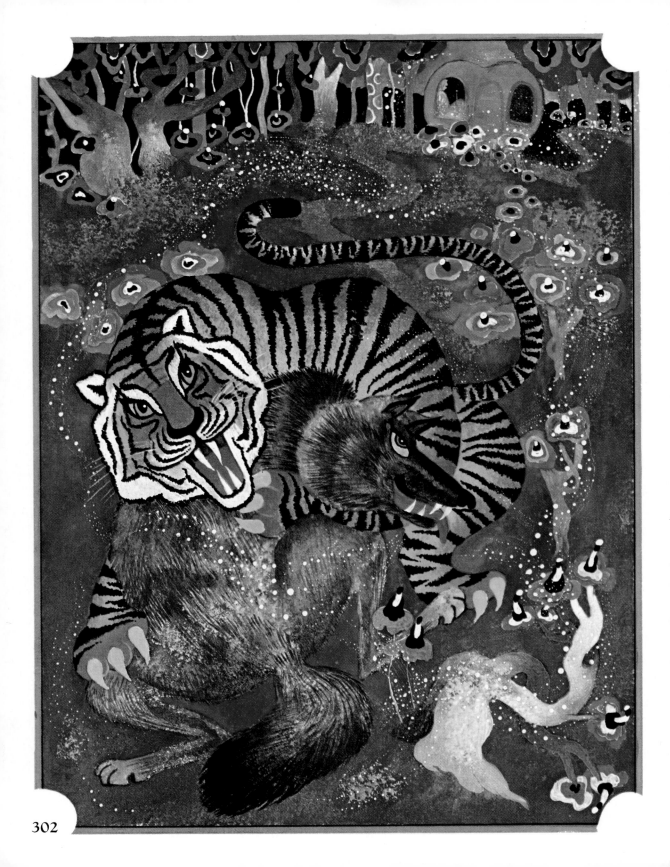

302

spun in a mad round of clawing, scratching, biting, and tearing.

Mother Parvati watched the melee for a few moments, her dark eyes dancing with mischief. Then she calmly said, *"Chal ra, Bhopalla, tunuk, tunuk."* With a rumble and a whir, the magic pumpkin rolled farther and farther away from the furious battle. At last the dark jungle was left behind, and the pumpkin rolled into the sunlit garden of wise Mother Parvati.

"Home at last!" she sighed, smiling as she stepped out of her magic pumpkin. "I never *did* intend to be anybody's dinner!"

## AUTHOR

Gloria Skurzynski was born in Pennsylvania and once worked for a steel company in Pittsburgh. She began writing books after she was inspired by some poems one of her daughters had written. Besides writing many articles and stories for magazines, Mrs. Skurzynski is also the author of two other books of folktales — *In a Bottle with a Cork on Top* and *Two Fools and a Faker*.

The author and her husband, an aerospace engineer, have five daughters and live in Salt Lake City, Utah.

# Coplas

People in villages in Spain often make up and sing short songs called *coplas*. These little folk songs can be about many different things. Here are some examples:

Tengo mi pecho de coplas,
Que parece un hormiguero;
Y unas a otras se dicen:
¡Yo quiero salir primero!

Al subir por la escalera,
Una pulga me picó,
La cogí de las orejas . . .
¡Buen puntapié me dio!

Aunque te digan pecosa,
Niña, no te sepa malo;
Que el cielo con sus estrellas
Está muy bien adornado.

Mira el cielo vestirse
De ricas telas,
De día, azul y blanco,
De noche, estrellas.

My heart is filled with coplas,
Like a swarming anthill;
And each says to the other:
Let me out first!

As I climbed the stairs,
A flea did bite me,
I caught it by the ears . . .
But what a kick it gave me!

Though they call you freckles,
Don't be insulted;
The sky with its stars
Is amply speckled.

See how the sky dresses
In rich fabric,
By day it wears white and blue,
At night, stars.

# The Sound of Words

Almost anyone can tell a story, but a good storyteller uses words that make the story come alive. As you read, you can almost see *and* hear what is happening. "The Magic Pumpkin" is full of sound words. These are words that imitate, or sound like, what they describe.

Turn to page 299 and find the following sentence: "'I don't sssssuppose it could be the sssssame old lady,' the tiger *hissed*." The word *hiss* sounds much like the noise a tiger — or any cat — makes when it is angry. The five *s*'s in *sssssuppose* and *sssssame* tell you to say the words so that they will sound like hissing.

In the next sentence on page 299, the wolf *growls* his answer. The word *growl* sounds much like the deep, throaty noise an animal makes. *Grrrreatly* is spelled with four *r*'s to make you think of a growling sound when you read it.

Turn to page 300. Can you find some more examples of sound words? There are several of them in this sentence: "The stillness of the jungle was filled with thuds, thumps, hisses, howls . . ." Each of the words at the end of this sentence sounds like a certain noise. You have already seen how *hiss* and *growl* do this.

Think about the rest of the sound words in the sentence you've just read on page 300. See if you can figure out how each one imitates the sound it stands for. Be sure to keep your *ears* open for sound words as you read. They help make stories lively and fun.

# Annie and the Old One

## by MISKA MILES

Annie's Navajo world was good — a world of rippling sand, of high copper-red bluffs in the distance, of the low mesa near her own snug hogan. The pumpkins were yellow in the cornfield, and the tassels on the corn were turning brown.

Each morning, the gate to the night pen near the hogan was opened wide, and the sheep were herded to pasture on the desert.

Annie helped watch the sheep. She carried pails of water to the cornfield. And every weekday, she walked to the bus stop and waited for the yellow bus that took her to school and brought her home again.

Best of all were the evenings when she sat at her grandmother's feet and listened to stories of times long gone.

---

Adapted from *Annie and the Old One* by Miska Miles. Published by Little, Brown and Company.

Sometimes it seemed to Annie that her grandmother was her age — a girl who had seen no more than nine or ten harvestings.

If a mouse scurried and jerked across the hard dirt floor of their hogan, Annie and her grandmother laughed together. And when they prepared the fried bread for the evening meal, if it burned a bit black at the edges, they laughed and said it was good.

There were other times when her grandmother sat small and still, and Annie knew that she was very old. Then Annie would cover the thin knees of the Old One with a blanket.

It was at such a time that her grandmother said, "It is time you learn to weave, my granddaughter."

Annie touched the web of wrinkles that crisscrossed her grandmother's face and slowly went outside the hogan.

Beside the door, her father sat cross-legged, working with silver and fire, making a handsome, heavy necklace. Annie passed him and went to the big loom where her mother sat weaving.

Annie sat beside the loom, watching, while her mother slid the weaving stick in place among the strings of the warp. With red wool, her mother added a row to a slanting arrow of red, bright against the dull background.

Annie's thoughts wandered. She thought about the stories her grandmother had told — stories of hardship when rains flooded the desert — of dry weather when rains did not fall and the pumpkins and corn were dry in the field.

Annie looked out across the sand where the cactus bore its red fruit and thought about the coyote guarding the scattered hogans of the Navajos.

Annie watched while her mother worked. She made herself sit very still.

After a time, her mother looked at her and smiled. "Are you ready to weave now, my daughter?"

Annie shook her head.

She continued to watch while her mother twisted the weaving stick in the warp, making a shed for the strands of gray and red wool.

At last her mother said softly, "You may go," almost as though she knew what Annie wanted.

Annie ran off to find her grandmother, and together they gathered twigs and brush to feed the small fire in the middle of the hogan.

When the evening meal was done, the old grandmother called her family together.

Annie and her mother and father stood quietly, respectfully, waiting for the grandmother to speak.

A coyote called shrilly from the mesa.

There was no sound in the hogan except a small snap of the dying fire.

Then the grandmother spoke softly.

"My children, when the new rug is taken from the loom, I will go to Mother Earth."

Annie shivered and looked at her mother.

Her mother's eyes were shining bright with tears that did not fall, and Annie knew what her grandmother meant. Her heart stood still, and she made no sound.

The Old One spoke again.

"You will each choose the gift that you wish to have."

Annie looked at the hard earth, swept smooth and clean.

"What will you have, my granddaughter?" the grandmother asked.

Annie looked at a weaving stick propped against the wall of the hogan. This was her grandmother's own weaving stick, polished and beautiful with age. Annie looked directly at the stick.

As though Annie had spoken, her grandmother nodded.

"My granddaughter shall have my weaving stick."

On the floor of the hogan lay a rug that the Old One had woven long, long ago. Its colors were soft, and its warp and weft were strong.

Annie's mother chose the rug.

Annie's father chose the silver and turquoise belt that was now loose around the small waist of the Old One.

Annie folded her arms tightly across her stomach and went outside, and her mother followed.

"How can my grandmother know she will go to Mother Earth when the rug is taken from the loom?" Annie asked.

"Many Old Ones know," her mother said.

"How do they know?"

"Your grandmother is one of those who live in harmony with all nature — with earth, coyote, birds in the sky. They know more than many will ever learn. Those Old Ones know." Her mother sighed deeply. "We will speak of other things."

In the days that followed, the grandmother went about her work as she had always done.

She ground corn to make meal for bread.

She gathered dry twigs and brush to make fire.

And when there was no school, she and Annie watched the sheep and listened to the sweet, clear music of the bell on the collar of the lead goat.

The weaving of the rug was high on the loom. It was almost as high as Annie's waist.

"My mother," Annie said, "why do you weave?"

"I weave so we may sell the rug and buy the things we must have from the trading post. Silver for silver-making. Deer hide for boots — "

"But you know what my grandmother said — "

Annie's mother did not speak. She slid her weaving stick through the warp and picked up a strand of rose-red wool.

Annie turned and ran. She ran across the sand and huddled in the shade of the small mesa. Her grandmother would go back to the earth when the rug was taken from the loom. The rug must not be finished. Her mother must not weave.

# A Part of the Earth

The next morning, where her grandmother went, Annie followed.

When it was time to go to the bus stop to meet the school bus, she dawdled, walking slowly and watching her feet. Perhaps she would miss the bus.

And then quite suddenly she did not want to miss it. She knew what she must do.

She ran hard, as fast as she could — breathing deeply — and the yellow bus was waiting for her at the stop.

She climbed aboard. The bus moved on, stopping now and then at hogans along the way. Annie sat there alone and made her plan.

In school, she would be bad, so bad that the teacher would have to send for her mother and father.

And if her mother and father came to school to talk to the teacher, that would be one day her mother could not weave. One day.

On the playground, Annie's teacher asked, "Who will lead the exercises today?"

No one answered.

The teacher laughed, "Very well. Then I shall be leader." The teacher was young, with yellow hair. Her blue skirt was wide and the heels on her brown shoes were high. The teacher kicked off her shoes, and the girls laughed.

Annie followed the teacher's lead — bending, jumping, and she waited for the time when the teacher would lead them in jogging around the playground.

As Annie jogged past the spot where the teacher's shoes lay on the ground, she picked up a shoe and hid it in the folds of her dress.

When Annie jogged past a trash can, she dropped the shoe inside.

Some of the girls saw her and laughed, but some frowned. When the line jogged near the schoolhouse door, Annie slipped from the line and went inside to her room and her own desk.

Clearly she heard the teacher as she spoke to the girls outside.

"The other shoe, please." Her voice was pleasant. Then there was silence.

Limping, one shoe on and one shoe gone, the teacher came into the room.

The girls followed, giggling and holding their hands across their mouths.

"I know it's funny," the teacher said, "but now I need the shoe."

Annie looked at the boards of the floor. A shiny black beetle crawled between the cracks.

The door opened, and another teacher came inside with a shoe in his hand. As he passed Annie's desk, he touched her shoulder and smiled down at her.

"I saw someone playing tricks," he said.

The teacher looked at Annie, and the room was very still.

When school was over for the day, Annie waited.

Timidly, with hammering heart, she went to the teacher's desk.

"Do you want my mother and father to come to the school tomorrow?" she asked.

"No, Annie," the teacher said. "I have the shoe. Everything is all right."

Annie's face was hot, and her hands were cold. She turned and ran. She was the last to climb on the bus.

Finally, there was her own bus stop. She

hopped down and slowly trudged the long way home. She stopped beside the loom.

The rug was now much higher than her waist.

That night she curled up in her blanket. She slept lightly and awakened before dawn.

There was no sound from her mother's sheepskin. Her grandmother was a quiet hump in her blanket. Annie heard only her father's loud, sleeping breathing. There was no other sound on the whole earth, except the howling of a coyote from far across the desert.

In the dim light of early morning, Annie crept outside to the night pen where the sheep were sleeping. The dry wood creaked when she undid the gate and pushed it wide open.

She tugged at the sleeping sheep until one stood quietly. Then the others stood also, uncertain — shoving together. The lead goat turned toward the open gate, and Annie slipped her fingers through his belled collar. She curled her fingertips across the bell, muffling its sound, and led the goat through the gate. The sheep followed.

She led them across the sand and around the small mesa where she released the goat.

"Go," she said.

She ran back to the hogan and slid under her blanket and lay shivering. Now her family would hunt the sheep all day. This would be the day when her mother would not weave.

When the fullness of morning came and it was light, Annie watched her grandmother rise and go outside.

Annie heard her call.

"The sheep are gone."

Annie's mother and father hurried outside, and Annie followed.

Her mother moaned softly, "The sheep — the sheep —— "

"I see them," the grandmother said. "They graze near the mesa."

Annie went with her grandmother, and when they reached the sheep, Annie's fingers slipped under the goat's collar, and the bell tinkled sharply as the sheep followed back to the pen.

In school that day, Annie sat quietly and wondered what more she could do. When the teacher asked questions, Annie looked at the floor. She did not even hear.

When night came, she curled up in her blanket, but not to sleep.

When everything was still, she slipped from her blanket and crept outside.

The sky was dark and secret. The wind was soft against her face. For a moment, she stood waiting until she could see in the night. She went to the loom.

She felt for the weaving stick there in its place among the warp strings. She separated the warp and felt for the wool.

Slowly she pulled out the strands of yarn, one by one.

One by one, she laid them across her knees.

And when the row was removed, she separated the strings of the warp again and reached for the second row.

When the woven rug was only as high as her waist, she crept back to her blanket, taking the strands of wool with her.

Under the blanket, she smoothed the strands and made them into a ball. And then she slept.

The next night, Annie removed another day's weaving. In the morning when her

mother went to the loom, she looked at the weaving — puzzled —

For a moment, she pressed her fingers against her eyes.

The Old One looked at Annie curiously. Annie held her breath.

The third night, Annie crept to the loom. A gentle hand touched her shoulder.

"Go to sleep, my granddaughter," the Old One said.

Annie wanted to throw her arms around her grandmother's waist and tell her why she had been bad, but she could only stumble to her blanket and huddle under it and let the tears roll into the edge of her hair.

When morning came, Annie unrolled herself from the blanket and helped prepare the morning meal.

Afterward, she followed her grandmother through the cornfield. Her grandmother walked slowly, and Annie fitted her steps to the slow steps of the Old One.

When they reached the small mesa, the Old One sat, crossing her knees and folding her gnarled fingers into her lap.

Annie knelt beside her.

The Old One looked far off toward the rim of desert where sky met sand.

"My granddaughter," she said, "you have tried to hold back time. This cannot be done." The desert stretched yellow and brown away to the edge of the morning sky. "The sun comes up from the edge of earth in the morning. It returns to the edge of earth in the evening. Earth, from which good things come for the living creatures on it. Earth, to which all creatures finally go."

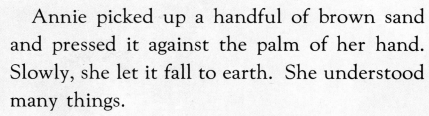

Annie picked up a handful of brown sand and pressed it against the palm of her hand. Slowly, she let it fall to earth. She understood many things.

The sun rose but it also set.

The cactus did not bloom forever. Petals dried and fell to earth.

She knew that she was a part of the earth and the things in it. She would always be a part of the earth, just as her grandmother had always been, just as her grandmother would always be, always and forever.

And Annie was breathless with the wonder of it.

They walked back to the hogan together, Annie and the Old One.

Annie picked up the old weaving stick. "I am ready to weave," she said to her mother. "I will use the stick that my grandmother has given me." She knelt at the loom.

She separated the warp strings and slipped the weaving stick in place, as her mother had done, as her grandmother had done.

She picked up a strand of gray wool and started to weave.

## AUTHOR

When Miska Miles was seven years old, she wrote a poem that was printed in a newspaper. Since then she has been an author, a poet, and a teacher. Under her real name, Patricia Miles Martin, and her pen name, Miska Miles, she has written many books.

*Annie and the Old One,* winner of several awards, was also chosen as a Newbery Medal Honor Book. Other books you might enjoy by this author are *Gertrude's Pocket, Beaver Moon,* and *Noisy Gander.*

# Descriptive Language

Some stories seem dull, and you may not pay much attention to them. Other stories seem alive with sights and sounds and feelings. Most of the time, stories are interesting because of the way in which the author uses words to describe what is happening.

The following sentences show three different ways of describing the same thing:

1. It was autumn in the forest.
2. Autumn was **a fire of bright colors** in the forest — golds like pieces of sunshine, deep reds, and warm oranges.
3. The autumn breeze brushed the brightly-colored leaves in the forest, making them whisper to each other as they **cut loose** and danced in the clear blue sky.

In sentence 1, you are told a simple fact — the season of the year in the forest. However, nothing has been added to the sentence to help you picture the colorful scene.

In sentence 2, you are given an idea of what the scene looked like. You are told about the bright colors you would see in the forest.

In sentence 3, you are told what you could see — the colorful, moving leaves and the blue sky. You are also told what you could hear — the sounds of the leaves.

When authors use words to help you paint a picture in your mind, they are using **descriptive language.** Descriptive language not only helps you picture what is going on, it can also give you certain feelings, which can make you feel happy or sad about what you are reading. An author may write, "The puppy sat on the front steps, its ears drooping, looking like it didn't have a friend in the world." The feeling you get is one of sadness. You feel the loneliness of the puppy.

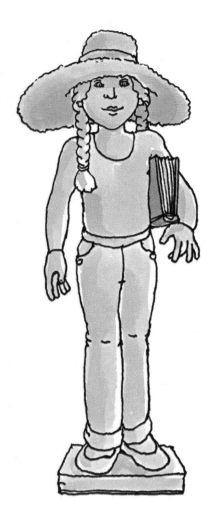

When you read descriptive language, make sure you understand what the author is telling you. An author may write, "Rita stood as still as a stone statue." Does the author mean that Rita was made of stone? No, that makes no sense. The author means that Rita stood still and did not move, just as a statue does not move. Many times, an author uses a group of words that means something quite different from what you might think. An author may write, "The tightrope-walker had the people in the audience on the edge of their seats." Does the author mean that the tightrope-walker made the people in the audience balance on the edge of their seats? No, that is not what is meant. The author means that the tightrope-walker made the people so excited that they sat forward in their seats. Look at the group of words in sentence 3 that are in heavy, dark print. Do these words mean exactly what they seem to say?

# REVIEW

1. Why do authors use descriptive language?
2. Look at the words in sentence 2 that are in heavy, dark print. Are they telling you that autumn is a fire? What are they telling you?
3. Which words in sentence 2 tell you about the color of the autumn leaves?
4. Which color in sentence 2 is compared to something else? To what is it compared?
5. Which words in sentence 3 tell you how the leaves sounded?
6. Look at the words in sentence 3 that are in heavy, dark print. What are they telling you?

## READING DESCRIPTIVE LANGUAGE

As you read the following story, notice the groups of words in heavy, dark print. Decide what they are telling you about what is happening in the story.

Barry awoke suddenly because **his alarm clock was screaming in his ear.** He pulled his arm out of the sleeping bag to shut it off.

The air felt so cold! **It was like putting his**

**arm into a bucket of ice-cold water.** Barry shut off the alarm and quickly drew his chilled arm back into the warm sleeping bag.

He knew there was a reason for getting up so early, but he could not quite remember what it was. **The reason was on the tip of his tongue.** Then he remembered. He and Aunt Maggie had to be up early today to go fishing!

He scrambled out of the sleeping bag and hurriedly got dressed. **He ran around the tent like a dog chasing rabbits.**

"Good morning, sleepyhead," Aunt Maggie called as Barry came out of the tent. "Come warm yourself by the fire while I make breakfast."

Barry crouched down next to the campfire. He loved to watch the fire. **The flames were brightly-colored ribbons, waving in the wind.**

"Well," said Aunt Maggie as she set a frying pan full of eggs on the fire, "are you looking forward to some fishing?"

"I sure am," Barry answered and **grinned from ear to ear.**

Magic
Words
to Feel
Better

A song of the Netsilik
by NAKASUK

SEA GULL
who flaps his wings
over my head
              in the blue air,
you GULL up there
dive down
              come here
take me with you
              in the air!
Wings flash by
my mind's eye
and I'm up there sailing
in the cool air,
              a-a-a-a-ah,
                    in the air.

335

from

# WINNIE-THE-POOH

by A.A. MILNE

# IN WHICH *Pooh and Piglet Go Hunting and Nearly Catch a Woozle*

The Piglet lived in a very grand house in the middle of a beech-tree, and the beech-tree was in the middle of the forest, and the Piglet lived in the middle of the house. Next to his house was a piece of broken board which had "TRESPASSERS W" on it. When Christopher Robin asked the Piglet what it meant, he said it was his grandfather's name and had been in the family for a long time. Christopher Robin said you *couldn't* be called Trespassers W, and Piglet said yes, you could, because his grandfather was, and it was short for Trespassers Will, which was short of Trespassers William. And his grandfather had had two names in case he lost one — Trespassers after an uncle, and William after Trespassers.

"I've got two names," said Christopher Robin carelessly.

"Well, there you are, that proves it," said Piglet.

One fine winter's day when Piglet was brushing away the snow in front of his house, he happened to look up, and there was Winnie-the-Pooh. Pooh was walking round and round in a circle, thinking of something else, and when Piglet called to him, he just went on walking.

"Hallo!" said Piglet. "What are *you* doing?"

"Hunting," said Pooh.

"Hunting what?"

"Tracking something," said Winnie-the-Pooh very mysteriously.

"Tracking what?" said Piglet, coming closer.

"That's just what I ask myself. I ask myself, What?"

"What do you think you'll answer?"

"I shall have to wait until I catch up with it," said Winnie-the-Pooh. "Now, look there." He pointed to the ground in front of him. "What do you see there?"

"Tracks," said Piglet. "Paw-marks." He gave a little squeak of excitement. "Oh, Pooh! Do you think it's a — a — a Woozle?"

"It may be," said Pooh. "Sometimes it is, and sometimes it isn't. You never can tell with paw-marks."

With these few words, he went on tracking, and Piglet, after watching him for a minute or

two, ran after him. Winnie-the-Pooh had come to a sudden stop and was bending over the tracks in a puzzled sort of way.

"What's the matter?" asked Piglet.

"It's a very funny thing," said Bear, "but there seem to be *two* animals now. This — whatever-it-was — has been joined by another — whatever-it-is — and the two of them are now proceeding in company. Would you mind coming with me, Piglet, in case they turn out to be Hostile Animals?"

Piglet scratched his ear in a nice sort of way, and said that he had nothing to do until Friday, and would be delighted to come, in case it really *was* a Woozle.

"You mean, in case it really is two Woozles,"

said Winnie-the-Pooh, and Piglet said that anyhow he had nothing to do until Friday. So off they went together.

There was a small spinney of larch trees just here, and it seemed as if the two Woozles, if that is what they were, had been going round this

spinney; so round this spinney went Pooh and Piglet after them; Piglet passing the time by telling Pooh what his Grandfather Trespassers W had done to Remove Stiffness after Tracking, and how his Grandfather Trespassers W had suffered in his later years from Shortness of Breath, and other matters of interest, and Pooh wondering what a Grandfather was like, and if perhaps this was Two Grandfathers they were after now, and if so, whether he would be allowed to take one home and keep it, and what Christopher Robin would say. And still the tracks went on in front of them. . . .

Suddenly Winnie-the-Pooh stopped and pointed excitedly in front of him. *"Look!"*

*"What?"* said Piglet with a jump. And then, to show that he hadn't been frightened, he jumped up and down once or twice in an exercising sort of way.

"The tracks!" said Pooh. *"A third animal has joined the other two!"*

"Pooh!" cried Piglet. "Do you think it is another Woozle?"

"No," said Pooh, "because it makes different marks. It is either Two Woozles and one, as it

might be, Wizzle, or Two, as it might be, Wizzles
and one, if so it is, Woozle.  Let us continue to
follow them."

So they went on, feeling just a little anxious
now, in case the three animals in front of them
were of Hostile Intent.  And Piglet wished very
much that his Grandfather T. W. were there,
instead of elsewhere, and Pooh thought how nice
it would be if they met Christopher Robin suddenly but quite accidentally, and only because he
liked Christopher Robin so much.  And then, all
of a sudden, Winnie-the-Pooh stopped again and
licked the tip of his nose in a cooling manner, for
he was feeling more hot and anxious than ever in
his life before. *There were four animals in front of
them!*

"Do you see, Piglet? Look at their tracks! Three, as it were, Woozles, and one, as it was, Wizzle. *Another Woozle has joined them!*"

And so it seemed to be. There were the tracks; crossing over each other here, getting muddled up with each other there; but, quite plainly every now and then, the tracks of four sets of paws.

"I *think*," said Piglet, when he had licked the tip of his nose, too, and found that it brought very little comfort, "I *think* that I have just re-membered something. I have just remembered something that I forgot to do yesterday and shan't be able to do tomorrow. So I suppose I really ought to go back and do it now."

"We'll do it this afternoon, and I'll come with you," said Pooh.

"It isn't the sort of thing you can do in the afternoon," said Piglet quickly. "It's a very par-ticular morning thing that has to be done in the morning, and if possible, between the hours of —— What would you say the time was?"

"About twelve," said Winnie-the-Pooh, looking at the sun.

"Between, as I was saying, the hours of twelve and twelve five. So, really, dear old Pooh, if you'll excuse me —— *What's that?*"

Pooh looked up at the sky, and then, as he heard the whistle again, he looked up into the branches of a big oak-tree, and then he saw a friend of his.

"It's Christopher Robin," he said.

"Ah, then you'll be all right," said Piglet. "You'll be quite safe with *him*. Good-by," and he trotted off home as quickly as he could, very glad to be Out of All Danger again.

Christopher Robin came slowly down his tree.

"Silly old Bear," he said, "what *were* you doing? First you went round the spinney twice by yourself, and then Piglet ran after you and you went round again together, and then you were just going round a fourth time —— "

"Wait a moment," said Winnie-the-Pooh, holding up his paw.

He sat down and thought, in the most thoughtful way he could think. Then he fitted his paw into one of the Tracks . . . and then he scratched his nose twice and stood up.

"Yes," said Winnie-the-Pooh.

"I see now," said Winnie-the-Pooh.

"I have been Foolish and Deluded," said he, "and I am a Bear of No Brain at All."

"You're the Best Bear in All the World," said Christopher Robin soothingly.

"Am I?" said Pooh hopefully. And then he brightened up suddenly.

"Anyhow," he said, "it is nearly Luncheon Time." So he went home for it.

# AUTHOR

A.A. Milne began to write *Winnie-the-Pooh* while watching his son, Christopher Robin, at play. The real Christopher Robin actually had a stuffed bear named Winnie-the-Pooh. Mr. Milne added other animals to his stories, such as Piglet, Eeyore the donkey, and Kanga and Baby Roo. He wrote four books about Christopher Robin and his friends. *Winnie-the-Pooh* and *The House at Pooh Corner* are collections of stories. *When We Were Very Young* and *Now We Are Six* are books of poems.

When these books first became famous, people were excited to learn that A.A. Milne really had a son named Christopher Robin. Some wrote letters to the little boy, and some even came to see him! Mr. Milne grew worried that his son would be spoiled by all the attention, so he decided not to write any more Christopher Robin books.

A.A. Milne was born in London in 1882 and died in 1956. For many years, he was an assistant editor of *Punch,* a humorous British magazine. He wrote many plays, poems, and stories for adults, but he is remembered most for his Christopher Robin books.

# A Rainbow of Feelings

Color — how dull our world would be without it. How dull our reading would be too! Color words not only help us to picture things, they also help us to feel things.

Reread the first paragraph of "Annie and the Old One" on page 308. What color words are used? Yes, the author talks of *copper-red* bluffs, *yellow* pumpkins, and the *brown* tassels on the corn. She has used color words to help you see the place where Annie lives. But these words are also meant to give you a certain kind of feeling. As you read the description, you can almost feel the sun shining down on the desert sand. This is just what the author wants. She wants you to feel the warmth of Annie's home and family.

Look at the following two sentences:

1. Marcy sat by the river, watching the cold, gray rain turn the water a muddy brown.

2. Kevin sat by the river, watching the sun sparkling yellow and gold as it danced on the water.

Which sentence gives you a happier feeling? Probably the second one. Yellow and gold are bright, warm colors. Gray and brown are rather dull and cold, not at all cheerful.

It's hard to say why certain colors give you certain kinds of feelings, but it's no secret that they do. Authors know that. That is why they choose the color words in their stories very carefully. They want you to feel, as well as see, what they write about. So as you read, keep that in mind. Open yourself to a rainbow of feelings.

# Books to Enjoy

**Ramona and Her Father** by Beverly Cleary
When her father loses his job, Ramona helps her family in funny yet serious ways.

**Railroad Arthur** by Alan Coren
This adventure story of the old West is full of humor as a boy tracks down train robbers.

**The Wentletrap Trap** by Jean George
On the island of Bimini, Dennis tries to get a rare and valuable shell.

**The Girl Who Loved Wild Horses**
by Paul Goble
A Plains Indian girl shares the life of a band of Western wild horses.

**Squeeze a Sneeze** by Bill Morrison
This book of nonsense rhymes will make you want to make up some of your own.

**The Magic Cooking Pot** by Faith Towle
An old folktale from India shows what happens when a poor man's magic pot is stolen.

# Glossary

# Glossary

This glossary can help you find out meanings and pronunciations of words in this book that you may not know. The meanings of the words as they are used in this book are always given. Often you will also find other common meanings listed.

You can find out the correct pronunciation of any glossary word by using the special spelling after the word and the pronunciation key. The *Full Pronunciation Key* below shows how to pronounce each consonant and vowel in a special spelling. There is also a short form of this full key at the bottom of every left-hand page in the glossary.

## *FULL PRONUNCIATION KEY*

**Consonant Sounds**

| | | | | | |
|---|---|---|---|---|---|
| b | bib | k | cat, kick | sh | ship, dish |
| ch | church | l | lid, needle | t | tight |
| d | did | m | man, am | th | thin, path |
| f | fast, off | n | no, sudden | *th* | this, bathe |
| g | gag | ng | thing | v | vine, cave |
| h | hat | p | pop | w | with |
| hw | which | r | roar | y | yes |
| j | judge | s | see, miss | z | zebra, size |
| | | | | zh | pleasure |

**Vowel Sounds**

| | | | | | |
|---|---|---|---|---|---|
| ă | pat | î | fierce, dear | ŭ | cut |
| ā | pay | ŏ | pot | û | turn, circle |
| â | air, care | ō | go | yōō | use |
| ä | father | ô | paw, for | ə | about, silent, |
| ĕ | pet | oi | noise, boy | | pencil, lemon, |
| ē | be | o͝o | took | | circus |
| ĭ | pit | o͞o | boot | ər | butter |
| ī | pie, by | ou | out, cow | | |

Pronunciation key and word meanings are adapted from *The American Heritage School Dictionary*, © 1972, 1977 by Houghton Mifflin Company.

## A

**a·ca·cia** (ə kā′shə) A kind of tree with yellow flowers and feathery leaves that grows mainly in warm places.

**ac·com·pa·ny** (ə kŭm′pə nē) To be with or go along with.

**ac·quaint·ance** (ə kwān′təns) A person whom one knows.

**ad·mi·ra·tion** (ăd mə rā′shən) Very great respect.

**ad·mire** (ăd mīr′) **1.** To look at with wonder or pleasure. **2.** To feel respect for.

**ad·mir·ing·ly** (ăd mīr′ĭng lē) In a manner showing pleasure or respect for.

**a·dor·a·ble** (ə dôr′ə bəl) Very charming or cute.

**an·ces·tor** (ăn′sĕs tər) Any relative from the past, especially one who lived before a grandparent.

**an·cient** (ān′shənt) Very old.

**an·noy·ance** (ə noi′əns) Displeasure: *We won the football game, much to the other team's annoyance.*

**an·noyed** (ə noid′) Displeased; angry.

**anx·ious** (ăngk′shəs) Uneasy; nervous.

**anx·ious·ly** (ăngk′shəs lē) In a nervous manner.

**ap·pe·tite** (ăp′ĭ tīt) The desire for food.

**a·ri·a** (är′ē ə) A piece of music for a solo singer.

**a·ro·ma** (ə rō′mə) A pleasant smell.

**as·ton·ished** (ə stŏn′ĭsht) Filled with wonder; surprised.

**as·ton·ish·ment** (ə stŏn′ĭshmənt) Great surprise; amazement; wonder.

**awn·ing** (ô′nĭng) A rooflike canvas screen set up as protection from sun or rain.

## B

**bab·bling** (băb′lĭng) Making a series of sounds that the hearer cannot understand.

**badg·er** (băj′ər) A burrowing animal with short legs and thick, grayish fur.

---

ă pat / ā pay / â care / ä father / ĕ pet / ē be / ĭ pit / ī pie / î fierce / ŏ pot / ō go
ô paw, for / oi noise / o͝o book / o͞o boot / ou out / ŭ cut / û turn / th thin / *th* this
    hw **which** / zh pleasure / ə about, silent, pencil, lemon, circus

**ba·sis** (bā′sĭs) The main part.

**bat·tered** (băt′ərd) Hurt by rough handling: *His car was badly battered.*

**beech** (bēch) A kind of nut tree.

**bees·wax** (bēz′wăks) **1.** The yellowish or brownish wax produced by honeybees for making their honeycombs. **2.** Of anything made from this wax, such as candles or crayons.

**be·hold** (bĭ hōld′) To see; to look at.

**bel·low** (bĕl′ō) To make a loud roaring noise.

**be·wil·der·ment** (bĭ wĭl′dər-mənt) A state of being greatly confused.

**bleach·ers** (blē′chərz) Uncovered bench seats for people watching outdoor sports.

**bluff**[1] (blŭf) **1.** To mislead. **2.** The act of misleading by a false show of strength.

**bluff**[2] (blŭf) A high, steep cliff.

**bom·bard·ing** (bŏm bärd′ĭng) Showering (someone else) with repeated talking: *The bombarding voices of reporters greeted the mayor when she arrived at the airport.*

**bound**[1] (bound) To move by leaping: *The deer bounded away.*

**bound**[2] (bound) A limit; boundary: *Her joy knew no bounds.*

**braise** (brāz) To brown (meat or vegetables) in fat and then cook over low heat in a covered container.

**bra·vo** (brä′vō) A word used to show enjoyment of someone's performance.

**bread·fruit** (brĕd′froōt) The large round fruit of a tropical tree having rough skin and a fleshy inside that is like bread when baked.

**bur·ro** (bûr′ō) *or* (boŏr′ō) *or* (bŭr′ō) A small donkey, usually used for riding or for carrying loads.

**bus·tle** (bŭs′əl) To hurry busily or excitedly: *The mechanics bustled about the airfield.*

## C

**cack·le** (kăk′əl) **1.** To make the shrill, broken sound of a hen. **2.** To laugh or speak with a sound that is like this.

**cal·cu·la·tion** (kăl kyə lā′shən) The act of finding or figuring out (an answer or result).

**calm·ly** (**kăm′**lē) In a quiet, un-excited manner.

**ca·per**[1] (**kā′**pər) A playful jump or hop. — **cut capers.** To jump around playfully.

**ca·per**[2] (**kā′**pər) A pickled flower bud used to season food.

**ca·ress** (kə **rĕs′**) To touch or stroke lovingly.

**cell** (sĕl) The smallest part of a living substance: *blood cell, brain cell. A single cell can be seen only under a microscope.*

**cel·lo** (**chĕl′**ō) A stringed musical instrument that looks like a large violin.

**cen·ti·pede** (**sĕn′**tə pēd) An animal with a wormlike body divided into many sections, each with a pair of legs.

**cer·e·mo·ny** (**sĕr′**ə mō nē) A special act performed in honor of something: *a wedding ceremony.*

**chap·let** (**chăp′**lĭt) A circle made of flowers, leaves, or berries that is worn on the head.

**choir** (kwīr) A singing group.

**close** (klōs) Near. — (klōz) **1.** To shut. **2.** To bring to an end. **3.** An enclosed area.

**clum·sy** (**klŭm′**zē) **1.** Without grace; awkward. **2.** Difficult to handle or use.

**co·bra** (**kō′**brə) A poisonous snake that lives in Africa and Asia.

**col·lard greens** (**kŏl′**ərd grēnz) A leafy vegetable that is like cabbage.

**com·bine** (kəm **bīn′**) To bring or come together; to join. — (**kom′**bīn) A machine that cuts, threshes, and cleans grain.

**com·mer·cial** (kə **mûr′**shəl) An advertisement that is on radio or television.

**com·mis·sion·er** (kə **mĭsh′**ə-nər) A person in charge of a governmental department: *a police commissioner.*

**com·mon** (**kŏm′**ən) **1.** Most widely known of its kind. **2.** Often **commons.** A piece of land belonging to or used by the whole community.

---

ă pat / ā **pay** / â **care** / ä father / ĕ **pet** / ē be / ĭ pit / ī **pie** / î fierce / ŏ **pot** / ō go
ô **paw, for** / oi **noise** / ōŏ book / ōō boot / ou **out** / ŭ cut / û turn / th **thin** / *th* this
hw **wh**ich / zh pleasure / ə **about, silent, pencil, lemon, circus**

**con·cert** (kŏn′sûrt) A perform-ance of music.

**con·fi·dence** (kŏn′fĭ dəns) Trust or faith: *He had a lot of confi-dence in his doctor.*

**con·stant** (kŏn′stənt) Happening over and over again.

**con·ven·ient** (kən **vēn′**yənt) Easy to reach.

**co·ri·an·der** (**kôr′**ē ăn dər) A plant with spicy seeds used as a seasoning.

**cre·ate** (krē **āt′**) To make.

**crop** (krŏp) **1.** The amount of cultivated plants grown or gathered in a single season or place. **2.** A group or quantity appearing at one time: *a crop of new ideas.*

### D

**daw·dle** (dôd′l) To move more slowly than necessary.

**de·ceiv·ing** (dĭ **sēv′**ĭng) Making (a person) believe something that is not true; misleading.

**de·lude** (dĭ **lōōd′**) To mislead; trick.

**de·mand** (dĭ **mănd′**) To ask in a forceful way.

**de·scend·ant** (dĭ **sĕn′**dənt) A person considered to have

certain people as ancestors: *He is a descendant of kings.*

**de·scent** (dĭ **sĕnt′**) Family origin: *She is of French descent.*

**des·ert**[1] (**dĕz′**ərt) A dry, bare re-gion, often covered with sand, having little or no vegetation.

**de·sert**[2] (dĭ **zûrt′**) To leave or abandon.

**de·sign** (dĭ **zīn′**) **1.** To make plans by means of sketches or draw-ings. **2.** A plan, drawing, or pattern.

**des·per·ate·ly** (**dĕs′**pər ĭt lē) In a way that shows one is willing to do almost anything because of a problem that seems hopeless.

**di·gest·ing** (dĭ **jĕst′**ĭng) *or* (dī-) Changing (food) into a form that can be used by the body.

**dis·as·ter** (dĭ **zăs′**tər) Great de-struction or bad luck.

**drear·y** (**drîr′**ē) Cheerless; gloomy: *a dreary January rain.*

**du·et** (dōō **ĕt′**) A musical piece performed by two people.

### E

**earth·en·ware** (**ûr′**thən wâr) Made of clay that has been hardened by heat.

**em•brace** (ĕm brās′) To hug.

**en•a•ble** (ĕn ā′bəl) To give the means or chance to do something: *Science has enabled us to reach the moon.*

**en•chant•er** (ĕn chănt′ər) A person in a story who can cast spells and perform magic.

**en•tan•gle** (ĕn tăng′gəl) To make tangled; mix together: *The fishing line is entangled.*

**en•trance**[1] (ĕn′trəns) The door or passageway through which one enters.

**en•trance**[2] (ĕn trăns′) To fill with wonder.

**ewe** (yo͞o) A female sheep.

**ex•as•per•a•ted** (ĭg zăs′pə rāt-ĭd) Very irritated.

**ex•cuse** (ĭk skyo͞oz′) To pardon; forgive. —(ĭk skyo͞os′) A reason or explanation.

**ex•pen•ses** (ĭk spĕn′səz) Costs that are the result of carrying out an activity.

**ex•pert** (ĕk′spûrt) Having great knowledge or skill.

**ex•pose** (ĭk spōz′) To uncover.

### F

**fang** (făng) A long, sharp tooth.

**fa•tal** (fāt′l) Causing ruin or death.

**fe•ro•cious** (fə rō′shəs) Very cruel and fierce.

**flab•ber•gast•ed** (flăb′ər găst-ĭd) Completely surprised and confused.

**flus•tered** (flŭs′tərd) Nervous, excited, or confused.

**fold**[1] (fōld) To bend together, double up, or crease so that one part lies over the other.

**fold**[2] (fōld) A pen for sheep or other farm animals.

**found**[1] (found) Past tense of *find*.

**found**[2] (found) To set up (something): *Booker T. Washington founded Tuskegee Institute.*

**foun•da•tion** (foun dā′shən) The base on which a structure stands.

**frail** (frāl) Not having a strong body; weak.

---

ă pat / ā pay / â care / ä father / ĕ pet / ē be / ĭ pit / ī pie / î fierce / ŏ pot / ō go
ô paw, for / oi noise / o͝o book / o͞o boot / ou out / ŭ cut / û turn / th thin / *th* this
hw which / zh pleasure / ə about, silent, pencil, lemon, circus

**fran·ti·cal·ly** (frăn′tĭk lē) In an excited and fearful manner.

**fuss** (fŭs) To complain.

### G

**gar·land** (gär′lənd) A chain of flowers worn as a necklace or headpiece.

**ghee** (gē) A type of butter used in India and in neighboring countries.

**glis·ten·ing** (glĭs′ən ĭng) Shining with reflected light; sparkling; gleaming.

**glit·ter·ing** (glĭt′ər ĭng) Sparkling with light that looks like a series of bright flashes: *The lake was glittering in the sunlight.*

**gnarled** (närld) Having knots and being no longer smooth: *People who do certain types of work with their hands all their lives are likely to have gnarled fingers when they grow old.*

**gra·cious·ness** (grā′shəs nəs) Kindness; charm.

**greed·i·ly** (grēd′ĭ lē) In a way showing that one wants more than one should have; hungrily.

**grim·ly** (grĭm′lē) In a displeased manner.

**grip** (grĭp) **1.** A tight hold. **2.** To hold tightly.

**groom** (gro͞om) *or* (gro͝om) **1.** A man just married or about to be married. **2.** A person who takes care of horses. **3.** To clean and brush horses.

### H

**har·vest** (här′vĕst) To gather (a crop).

**haunch** (hônch) The hip and upper leg of an animal.

**hi·bis·cus** (hī bĭs′kəs) A tropical plant with large, showy, variously colored flowers.

**High·lands** (hī′ləndz) A mountainous area of northern and western Scotland.

**ho·gan** (hō′gôn) An earth-covered Navajo home.

**hoist·ing** (hoist′ĭng) The act of raising up, often with the help of some mechanical device.

**hon·ey·suck·le** (hŭn′ē sŭk əl) A type of vine with sweet-smelling flowers.

**hos·pi·tal·i·ty** (hŏs pĭ tăl′ĭ tē) Kind treatment of guests.

**hos·tile** (hŏs′təl) Unfriendly.

**hu·mil·i·at·ing** (hyo͞o mĭl′ē āt-ĭng) Very embarrassing.

**hurl** (hûrl) To throw with great force.

**I**

**ig·nore** (ĭg nôr′) To pay no attention to.

**im·me·di·ate·ly** (ĭ mē′ dē ĭt lē) At once.

**im·pu·dent** (ĭm′pyə dənt) Bold and often rude: *The child was punished for making an impudent remark to the adults.*

**in·quire** (ĭn kwīr′) To ask.

**in·tent** (ĭn tĕnt′) Purpose.

**in·ter·rupt** (ĭn tə rŭpt′) **1.** To break in and start to speak while someone else is still talking. **2.** To make (something) stop for a while: *The rain interrupted our game for an hour.*

**isle** (īl) An island, especially a small one.

**J**

**jo·ta** (hō′tä) A lively Spanish dance.

**ju·ni·per** (joō′nə pər) An evergreen tree or bush with prickly leaves and bluish berries.

**K**

**ker·o·sene lamp** (kĕr′ə sēn lămp) A lamp that is lit by kerosene, a thin, light-colored oil used as a fuel.

**knack·wurst** (nŏk′wûrst) A short, thick sausage.

**knelt** (nĕlt) Past tense of *kneel.*

**L**

**lank·y** (lăng′kē) Tall and thin.

**larch** (lärch) A tree in the pine family.

**leg·end** (lĕj′ənd) A story handed down from earlier times and that may or may not be based on fact.

**loathe** (lōth) To greatly dislike.

**loom**[1] (loōm) **1.** To come into view as a large, often unclear, image: *Clouds loomed behind the mountains.* **2.** To seem close at hand: *The day of the test loomed before us.*

---

ă pat / ā pay / â care / ä father / ĕ pet / ē be / ĭ pit / ī pie / î fierce / ŏ pot / ō go
ô paw, for / oi noise / oŏ book / oō boot / ou out / ŭ cut / û turn / th thin / *th* this
hw which / zh pleasure / ə about, silent, pencil, lemon, circus

**loom²** (lo͞om) A frame on which yarn or thread is woven to make cloth.

**lus·trous** (lŭs′trəs) Gleaming; shiny.

# M

**ma·ha·ra·ja** (mä hə rä′jə) In olden times, a prince or king of India.

**man·ger** (mān′jər) An open box in which feed for horses or cattle is placed.

**man·go** (măng′gō) A yellow-orange fruit that is juicy and sweet-tasting.

**mar·i·gold** (măr′ĭ gōld) A garden plant with showy orange, yellow, or reddish flowers.

**ma·zur·ka** (mə zûr′kə) **1.** A lively Polish dance. **2.** A piece of music written for this dance.

**me·lee** (mā′lā) *or* (mā lā′) A fight filled with confusion.

**me·sa** (mā′sə) A hill with steep sides and a flat top.

**me·tal·lic** (mə tăl′ĭk) Sharp in sound, like metal being struck.

**mock** (mŏk) To make fun of.

**moor** (mo͝or) A large stretch of open land, often with marshy areas.

**mo·tion** (mō′shən) To make a signal, often with a hand.

**mud·dle** (mŭd′l) **1.** To get mixed up or confused. **2.** A mess.

**muf·fle** (mŭf′əl) To cover in order to make less noise.

**muf·fler** (mŭf′lər) A scarf worn around the neck for warmth.

**mus·cle** (mŭs′əl) Any one of the many parts of the body that cause bodily movement.

**must·y** (mŭs′tē) Stale and damp: *a musty smell.*

# N

**niche** (nĭch) **1.** A hollowed-out part of a wall, often used for holding a statue. **2.** A narrow crack, as in a rock.

**nuz·zle** (nŭz′əl) To push gently with the nose: *The calf nuzzled its mother.*

# O

**ob·ject¹** (ŏb′jĭkt) **1.** A thing that has shape and can be seen. **2.** A purpose; goal.

**ob·ject²** (əb jĕkt′) To argue; protest.

**or·na·ment** (ôr′nə mənt) Something that is worn or used as a decoration.

## P

**pal·met·to** (păl mĕt′ō) A small palm tree with fan-shaped leaves.

**pang** (păng) A sudden, sharp feeling of fear, sadness, or pain.

**per·fect** (pûr′fĭkt) **1.** Completely suited. **2.** Without faults or mistakes. — (pər fĕkt′) To make excellent.

**per·ish** (pĕr′ĭsh) To die.

**per·ish·a·ble** (pĕr′ĭ shə bəl) Likely to spoil. — **perishables.** Things, such as food, that spoil easily.

**pierc·ing** (pîr′sĭng) Sharp; penetrating: *piercing cold.*

**plaque** (plăk) A flat plate, sometimes used as a sign on a monument or statue.

**plod** (plŏd) To walk heavily or with great effort.

**pluck** (plŭk) **1.** To pick: *pluck a flower.* **2.** To pull; tug: *pluck a sleeve.* **3.** Courage and daring. — **pluck up.** To gather up.

**plump** (plŭmp) Full; fleshy; rounded.

**pot·sie squares** (pŏt′sē skwârz) The numbered spaces that are used to play hopscotch.

**pre·cious** (prĕsh′əs) Highly prized or valued.

**pro·ceed** (prō sēd′) To go forward or onward.

**pro·file** (prō′fīl) The outline (of something).

**prof·it** (prŏf′ĭt) The money made in an activity after all other costs have been met.

**prompt·ly** (prŏmpt′lē) In a quick and firm manner.

**pul·ley** (pool′ē) A device used to pull things, made up of a wheel with a groove around it through which a rope or cable runs.

## Q

**qua·ver·y** (kwā′vər ē) Shaky.

**queue** (kyoo) **1.** A line of people awaiting a turn, as at a ticket window. **2.** A long pigtail.

---

ă pat / ā pay / â care / ä father / ĕ pet / ē be / ĭ pit / ī pie / î fierce / ŏ pot / ō go
ô paw, for / oi noise / oŏ book / oō boot / ou out / ŭ cut / û turn / th thin / *th* this
hw which / zh pleasure / ə about, silent, pencil, lemon, circus

## R

**raf·fi·a** (răf′ē ə) Fiber, or strands, from the leaves of a certain palm tree used for baskets and other things.

**ra·tel** (rät′l) *or* (rāt′l) An animal of Africa and Asia, having short legs and thick fur.

**re·cit·al** (rĭ sīt′l) A musical performance, usually by one person.

**re·frain** (rĭ frān′) To keep oneself from doing something: *I try to refrain from eating too much candy.*

**re·fuse**[1] (rĭ fyōōz′) To turn down; not accept.

**ref·use**[2] (rĕf′yōōs) Worthless matter; waste.

**re·hearse** (rĭ hûrs′) To practice for a performance.

**rein** (rān) **1.** Often **reins.** The strap that is attached to the bit in a horse's mouth and held by the rider to direct and control the horse. **2.** To stop (one's horse) by pulling on the reins.

**ren·der** (rĕn′dər) To give or provide: *Our business always renders prompt service.*

**res·o·nance** (rĕz′ə nəns) A full, pleasing sound, especially that of a musical instrument or voice.

**re·spect·ful·ly** (rĭ spĕkt′fəl ē) Showing politeness: *He bowed respectfully to the audience.*

**re·spec·tive** (rĭ spĕk′tĭv) Having to do with each of two or more people or things: *The school bus dropped the children off at their respective homes.*

**re·us·a·ble** (rē yōō′zə bəl) Able to be used again.

**rhythm** (rĭth′əm) **1.** A regular repeating of a beat, as in music. **2.** A pattern of beats, as in poetry when read aloud.

**rock garden.** A rocky area in which plants and flowers that can grow there are planted.

## S

**sa·ri** (sä′rē) A gownlike garment worn by women in India.

**scent** (sĕnt) A smell.

**scone** (skōn) A soft and doughy biscuit.

**scur·ry** (skûr′ē) To run about hurriedly.

**sep·a·rate** (sep′ə rāt) To take apart or keep apart. — (sĕp′ə rĭt) *or* (sĕp′rĭt) Single; not together; by itself.

**shan't** (shănt) Shall not.

**shed** (shĕd) A triangular opening made between raised and lowered crosswise threads through which the weaving stick is passed.

**short•bread** (**shôrt′**brĕd) A dough of flour, sugar, and butter, rolled thickly, cut into cookies, and baked.

**shril•ly** (**shrĭl′**ē) Making a high-pitched and rather loud noise: *The siren screamed shrilly.*

**shriv•el** (**shrĭv′**əl) To shrink and wrinkle.

**sin•is•ter** (**sĭn′**ĭ stər) Suggesting something evil or frightening: *The full moon made sinister shadows in the graveyard.*

**skull** (skŭl) The bony framework of the head.

**snatch** (snăch) To steal.

**snooze** (sno͞oz) To take a light nap; doze.

**so•na•ta** (sə **nä′**tə) Any of several types of musical pieces, especially one that is written in several different movements, or parts.

**sooth•ing•ly** (**so͞o′**<i>th</i>ĭng lē) In a comforting manner.

**spi•nal cord** (**spī′**nəl kôrd) The central nerve that runs inside the backbone from the brain and branches off below into smaller nerves.

**spin•ney** (**spĭn′**ē) A thicket of small bushes or trees.

**splen•did** (**splĕn′**dĭd) Very striking to the eye; grand.

**sprang** (sprăng) Jumped up.

**sprout** (sprout) **1.** To begin to grow. **2.** A young plant growth, such as a bud or shoot.

**stern** (stûrn) Grave and serious.

**stern•ly** (**stûrn′**lē) In a serious manner.

**strand** (strănd) A single, string-like piece, often with other pieces: *That rope has three strands twisted together.*

**stut•ter** (**stŭt′**ər) To stumble over one's words because of nervousness or excitement.

---

ă pat / ā pay / â care / ä father / ĕ pet / ē be / ĭ pit / ī pie / î fierce / ŏ pot / ō go
ô paw, for / oi noise / o͝o book / o͞o boot / ou out / ŭ cut / û turn / th thin / *th* this
hw which / zh pleasure / ə about, silent, pencil, lemon, circus

**sub·sti·tute** (**sŭb′**stĭ to͞ot) *or* (-tyo͞ot) Someone or something that takes the place of another; a replacement.

**sub·way** (**sŭb′**wā) An underground railroad system found in some large cities.

**su·per** (**so͞o′**pər) Short form of **superintendent.**

**su·per·in·ten·dent** (so͞o pər-ĭn **tĕn′**dənt) A person who is in charge of a building.

**sur·viv·al** (sər **vī′**vəl) The act of staying alive.

**sur·vi·vor** (sər **vī′**vər) A person who has lived through an accident or disaster that caused the death of others.

**sus·pect** (sə **spĕkt′**) **1.** To consider (someone) possibly guilty. **2.** To have doubts about. — (**sŭs′**pĕkt) A person who is believed to have committed a crime.

**sym·bi·o·sis** (sĭm bī **ō′**sĭs) The relationship of two or more different creatures living closely together, often, but not always, to the benefit of each.

**sym·pho·ny or·ches·tra** (**sĭm′**-fə nē **ôr′**kĭ strə) A large group of musicians suited for playing symphonies, which are pieces of music usually written with four movements, or parts.

### T

**tan·go** (**tăng′**gō) A kind of Latin American dance.

**tang·y** (**tăng′**ē) Having a sharp flavor, taste, or smell.

**task** (tăsk) A job or duty.

**tas·sel** (**tăs′**əl) **1.** A bunch of string or thread tied at one end and hanging free at the other, used as a decoration. **2.** Something looking like this decoration, such as the group of flowers on a corn plant.

**tat·tered** (**tăt′**ərd) Torn or ragged.

**thatch** (thăch) **1.** Straw or leaves used to make a roof. **2.** To cover a house with straw or leaves.

**tim·id·ly** (**tĭm′**ĭd lē) In a shy, frightened manner.

**tor·rent** (**tôr′**ənt) A very forceful, strong rain.

**tra·di·tion·al** (trə **dĭsh′**ən əl) Passed along in a particular family or country as part of a culture: *the traditional Thanksgiving Day turkey.*

**tram·ple** (trăm′pəl) To step heavily, causing damage to whatever is underfoot.

**trem·ble** (trĕm′bəl) **1.** To shake, as from fear or cold. **2.** To vibrate.

**tre·men·dous** (trĭ mĕn′dəs) Very large or loud.

**tres·pass·er** (trĕs′pəs ər) *or* (-păs ər) One who goes onto someone else's property or anywhere one shouldn't be.

**tri·pod** (trī′pŏd) An object with three legs that holds something off the ground.

**trudge** (trŭj) To walk in a slow, heavy-footed manner.

**tu·a·ta·ra** (tōō ə tär′ə) A lizard-like animal of New Zealand.

**tur·quoise** (tûr′koiz) *or* (-kwoiz) A blue-green mineral often used in making jewelry, ornaments, and belts.

### U
**un·bolt** (ŭn bōlt′) To unlock.

**un·rav·el** (ŭn răv′əl) **1.** To separate (entangled threads) into single loose threads. **2.** To undo (a knitted fabric).

### W
**waltz** (wôlts) **1.** A type of dance. **2.** A piece of music, with three beats to the measure, that goes along with this dance.

**warp** (wôrp) In weaving, the threads that run along the length of a piece of cloth and are crossed by the weft.

**waste·land** (wāst′lănd) A lonely, usually empty place, such as a desert.

**wa·ter·works** (wô′tər wûrks) *or* (wŏt′ər-) The water system of a city or town.

**weft** (wĕft) In weaving, the crosswise threads that run between the warp threads. Also called **woof.**

**wir·y** (wīr′ē) Small and slim, but not necessarily weak.

---

ă pat / ā pay / â care / ä father / ĕ pet / ē be / ĭ pit / ī pie / î fierce / ŏ pot / ō go
ô paw, for / oi noise / ŏŏ book / ōō boot / ou out / ŭ cut / û turn / th **thin** / th **this**
hw **which** / zh pleasure / ə **about, silent, pencil, lemon, circus**

**Y**

**yacht** (yät) A small sailboat or motor boat used for racing and pleasure trips.

**Z**

**zin·ni·a** (zĭn′ē ə) A garden plant with showy, variously colored flowers.

"The Queen's Flowers," from *The Golden Goose and Other Plays*, by Fan Kissen. Copyright © 1963. Reprinted by permission of Houghton Mifflin Company.

"Snow," three haiku from *Flower Moon Snow: A Book of Haiku*, by Kazue Mizumura. Copyright © 1977 by Kazue Mizumura. Reprinted by permission of Thomas Y. Crowell.

"Something Strange Is Going On," adapted from *Something Queer Is Going On*, by Elizabeth Levy. Copyright © 1973 by Elizabeth Levy. Reprinted by permission of Delacorte Press.

"A Toad for Tuesday," adapted excerpt from *A Toad For Tuesday*, by Russell E. Erickson. Text copyright © 1974 by Russell E. Erickson. Used by permission of Lothrop, Lee & Shepard Co., a Division of William Morrow & Company.

"Unusual Friendships," from *Symbiosis: A Book of Unusual Friendships*, by Jose Aruego. Copyright © 1970 by Jose Aruego. Reprinted by permission of Charles Scribner's Sons.

"Your Busy Brain," from *Your Busy Brain*, by Louise Greep McNamara and Ada Bassett Litchfield. Text copyright © 1973 by Louise Greep McNamara and Ada Bassett Litchfield. Used by permission of Little, Brown and Company.

# Credits

*Illustrators:* pp. 10–24, LARRY JOHNSON; p. 25, BRUCE COCHRAN; pp. 26–38, DIANE DAWSON; p. 41, DIANE PATERSON; pp. 43–61, MARGARET HATHAWAY; pp. 62, 63, TERRY ALLEN; pp. 64–70, ALIKI BRANDENBERG; pp. 71–79, RUTH BRUNNER-STROSSER; pp. 82–93, JUDITH GOETEMANN; pp. 95, 96, 99, DIANE PATERSON; pp. 100–122, ROBERT BYRD; p. 123, TERRY ALLEN; pp. 130–150, EMILY MCCULLY; pp. 151–157, JOHN DAWSON; p. 158, MARVIN SIMMONS; pp. 161, 162, DIANE PATERSON; p. 165, KAZUE MIZUMURA; pp. 166–181, JULIE DOWNING; pp. 182, 183, TERRY ALLEN; pp. 184–197, SALLEY MAVOR; pp. 198–200, DOROTHEA SIERRA; pp. 201–212, SUSAN SPELLMAN MOHN; pp. 213, 214, 216–217, DIANE PATERSON; pp. 218–219, SUE THOMPSON; pp. 220–234, LEONARD LUBIN; Border: CAROL LACOURSE; p. 235, TERRY ALLEN; pp. 242–258, ARNOLD DOBRIN; pp. 259–263, JAMES CONNOLLY; p. 265, AL HIRSCHFELD drawing from The Margo Feiden Galleries, New York City; pp. 267, 269, DIANE PATERSON; pp. 271–283, GAIL OWENS; pp. 284–287, JOSE ARUEGO/ARIANE DEWEY; pp. 288–303, KRYSTYNA STASIAK; p. 306, TERRY ALLEN; pp. 308–328, JOE JACQUA; pp. 330, 331, 333, DIANE PATERSON; pp. 334–335, DOROTHEA SIERRA; pp. 336–346, ERNEST H. SHEPARD; p. 347, TERRY ALLEN.

*Photographers:* pp. 80–81, DENNIS STOCK/Magnum; p. 154, COURTESY VIRGINIA STATE LIBRARY; p. 198, UPI PHOTO; pp. 304–305, SANFORD/DPI.

*Book cover, title page, and magazine covers by* PAT WONG.